LIVING EVERY DAY WITH THE CROSS

LIVING EVERY DAY WITH THE CROSS

UNDERSTANDING THE
CONCEPT OF
FOLLOWING ALL THE
WAY

Aigbefo D. Ehihi

Aishific
- p r e s s -

Unless otherwise indicated, all Scripture quotations are taken from the Holy Bible, New Living Translation, copyright © 1996, 2004, 2015 by Tyndale House Foundation. Used by permission of Tyndale House Publishers, Carol Stream, Illinois 60188. All rights reserved.

Hardback ISBN: 979-8-9860017-2-2
Paperback ISBN: 979-8-9860017-6-0
eBook ISBN: 979-8-9860017-3-9
Library of Congress Control Number: 2024902307
Published by Aishific Press.
Aishific Press
Visit www.aisificpress.com.
books@aishific.com
1 (352) 300 6373
Printed in the United States of America.
Printed 2024.

Contents

INTRODUCTION   1

Section One   **5**
_____

One
WHAT IS DISCIPLESHIP?   7

Two
THE CRITICAL ELEMENTS OF GENUINE
FOLLOWERSHIP   16

Three
THE LEADING TEMPTATIONS OF A DISCIPLE   32

Four
THE ROLE OF THE WORD IN DISCIPLESHIP   69

Five
THE ROLE OF POLITICS IN A CHRISTIAN'S
LIFE   79

Section Two   **91**
_____

Six
A DISCIPLE IS OBEDIENT   93

Seven
A DISCIPLE IS MISSIONAL   104

Eight
A DISCIPLE IS A MULTIPLIER   126

Nine
A DISCIPLE IS COMMUNAL   146

Ten
A DISCIPLE IS A HUMBLE SERVANT   166

Eleven
A DISCIPLE IS A GOOD STEWARD   182

Twelve
A DISCIPLE IS SPIRITUALLY DISCIPLINED   195

Section Three   **211**

Thirteen
ASSESSMENT   212

Fourteen
ANALYSIS OF ASSESSMENT RESULTS   225

Fifteen
STEPS TO STAYING CLOSER TO GOD   232

REFERENCES   239

To my dad,
the Honorable Deacon Stephen O. Ehihi.

ACKNOWLEDGMENTS

I am immensely grateful to my wife for her unwavering patience and inspiration throughout the writing of this book. I would also like to express my thanks to my children, whose presence brought moments of joy during the writing process.

INTRODUCTION

> Christ does not need you to fake it till you make it, and He is not in the business of recruiting performers or cheerleaders. He is calling you to be His faithful followers.

Go therefore and make disciples of all nations, baptizing them in the name of the Father and of the Son and the Holy Spirit, teaching them to observe all that I have commanded you; and lo, I am with you always, to the close of the age (Matt 28:19–20). Those are the very words of the One who came, died for us, and is now preparing a place for us to join Him in heaven. From this command came this notion of discipleship. Careful exegesis helps us understand that the Church is called to train, equip, and deploy disciples. If we agree that discipleship is the local church's goal, we must articulate the essential traits that disciples should exhibit and their chosen suffering through the daily walk of life. This book seeks to help you live every day with your cross while still going about your daily business. It is based on biblical teachings and spiritual insights and offers a comprehensive guide to discipleship. It is grounded in biblical teachings and spiritual insights, providing a modern guide to discipleship.

The passage "Whoever wants to be my disciple must first deny themselves, take up their cross daily, and follow me" (Lk 9:23) drives every aspect of the book's discussion. This passage is this book's foundation and center of gravity, and I encourage you to hold it close to your heart and meditate on it as you consume this manuscript. We will spend more time interpreting and explaining its implications and its applications to followership later. The food for thought in each chapter will stir your appetite for the subject matter. At the same time, the thought-provoking self-reflection at the end of each chapter will reveal the aspects that require the Holy Spirit's immediate action.

This book is divided into three sections, each focusing on a critical aspect of discipleship. The first section covers the foundational elements of genuine followership, providing guidance for navigating the challenges that disciples face today. The second section explores the traits of a true disciple. Each chapter in this section expands on the vital features of discipleship, helping you separate the wheat from the chaff. This section also offers practical advice on obedience, faithfulness, missional living, communal engagement, humility in service, the ability to multiply, and effective stewardship. This section is a wealth of biblical wisdom and practical insights, helping readers understand what living as a true disciple of Christ means. The third section provides spiritual self-assessment tools and instructions on developing a personalized spiritual growth plan, enabling you to translate the book's teachings into actionable steps for your spiritual journey.

One of the critical questions this book asks is whether you desire to follow Christ all the way for the rest of your life. Is that desire robust enough to deny yourself, carry your cross, and follow Him daily? For those who claim to be His disciples, do they possess the essential characteristics of a true disciple, as outlined in this book? The book discusses what being a disciple means and how to follow Christ faithfully all the way, presenting the essential characteristics that should be evident in one who claims to be a disciple of Jesus.

As a proper takeoff technique, it is best to define the term "discipleship." Understanding this concept will help you grasp the essential characteristics of discipleship and how to live every day with the cross. Christ does not want anyone to fake it till they make it. He is not in the business of recruiting performers or cheerleaders. Instead, just as He called the disciples by the Sea of Galilee, Christ is calling you to be His true disciple. This call demands living a life of true worship, constantly seeking to worship Him in spirit and truth in every aspect of life. I hope this book helps you undertake the journey of discipleship to the point where it reflects in every aspect of your life.

Section One

WHAT IS CHRISTIAN
DISCIPLESHIP?

Food For Thought

Discipleship is more than having good knowledge of Christ; it is the action and commitment to following Him all the way with everything you've got.

One

WHAT IS DISCIPLESHIP?

> *Whoever wants to be my disciple must first deny themselves, take their cross daily, and follow me.*
>
> **Luke 9:23**

B eing a Christian is not about pledging membership to a society or union, paying monthly dues, or wearing the necessary religious accessories. It is not about Christian slogans, wearing faith T-shirts or wristbands, or posting hashtags. Neither is it about faking it until you make it. Christianity is not about performing, entertainment, or cheerleading. Christ is not looking for Christians like the Sadducees, who were the wealthy upper class mainly involved with the priesthood. They were famous for maintaining the temple's purity and making sacrifices at the temple. Their lives revolved around the temple, yet they never accepted Christ as their Savior.

God isn't looking for legalists like the Pharisees, whose lives revolve around teaching and keeping the law. The Pharisees were the most numerous and influential religious sects of Jesus's day. They stood for rigid observance of the law and traditions. Some good religious men were among them, but for the most part, they were known for covetousness, self-righteousness, and hypocrisy. What, then, does it mean to be a Christian? It means having a personal relationship with Christ, accepting Him as Lord and Savior, and following His teachings.

Christ referred to the Pharisees and the Sadducees as a brood of vipers. The Pharisees significantly influenced the masses and were highly esteemed during Christ's time. However, they were also known to be dishonest and unjust. In one of His parables, Jesus disapproved of the Pharisees' actions. The parable goes like this: Two men went to the temple to pray. One was a Pharisee, and the other a tax collector. The Pharisee stood up and prayed about himself, saying, "God, I thank you that I am not like other men, robbers, evildoers, adulterers, or even like this tax collector. I fast twice weekly and give a tenth of all I get."

Meanwhile, the tax collector stood at a distance, unable to look up to heaven. He beat his chest and said, "God, have mercy on me, a sinner." Jesus concluded that the tax collector, rather than the Pharisee, went home justified before God. He warned that those who exalt themselves like the Pharisee will be humbled, but those who humble themselves like the tax collector will be exalted (Lk 18:9–14, paraphrased).

As a Jewish sect, the Pharisees did an excellent job teaching and preserving God's Word. However, they missed out on its most significant benefit for themselves. This was because they lacked the humility required to embrace their long-awaited Messiah, and their self-righteousness deprived them of the salvific revelation before them. They missed the golden opportunity to become followers of Christ. So, what does it mean to be a follower of Christ?

First, a follower of Christ is someone who is called out and grounded in the basics of the Christian faith and capable of raising and nurturing new converts. The word "disciple" means a lifelong learner, a follower, an apprentice, or someone who commits to a life of learning and following. It is more than having good knowledge of Christ; it is the action and commitment to following Him all the way with everything you have. It is a continuous learning process that changes a person's life.

Furthermore, discipleship means committing to carrying your cross daily and following Jesus against all odds. Jesus made this definition simple enough when He said, "Whoever desires to be my disciple must deny themselves and take up their cross daily and follow me" (Lk 9:23). This passage is part of Christ's teachings, highlighting the commitment required to follow Him. He also emphasizes four critical elements of true discipleship, which is worthy of our in-depth discussion.

This definition from Jesus helps us understand that disciples do not get to choose their causes, purpose, values, or direction. He clarifies that "whoever does not carry his cross and follow Him cannot be His disciple, no more, no less (Lk 14:27). Although disciples are called, they are never coerced or exploited. They decide to carry the cross for the rest of their life, following Christ against all odds, enduring, and enjoying everything that comes with being a follower of Christ. Let's go back in time to understand the historical picture of discipleship through the lens of Christian spirituality.

Historically, "the origins of Christian spirituality lie in the scriptures—particularly in the New Testament."[1] It is believed that for the first five centuries of the Church, the human condition, the specific doctrines about God, and the world were well defined and could be understood in relationship to various patterns of the Christian life.[2] Therefore, all Christian spiritual traditions are rooted in scripture. The Jewish scriptures have played a substantial role in Christian spirituality for about two thousand years, from the benefit of the Book of Psalms in liturgy and the Song of Songs in mystical-contemplative writings to the role of the Book of Exodus in late-twentieth-century spiritualities of liberation.[3] From this essential scriptural background, the image of Christian spirituality is simply discipleship.

The concept of discipleship became interchangeable with leading or living a Christian life for all intents and purposes across two millennia at some point in the later history of Christian spirituality.[4] As Philip Sheldrake explains, the notion of discipleship has two related elements. The first is a call to conversion in response to God's incoming reign. "The time is fulfilled, and God's kingdom has come near; repent and believe in the good news" (Mk 1:15). The second dimension of discipleship is that of following the way of Jesus, which is both to adopt a way of life and to join in the work of building the Kingdom of God.[5] "And Jesus said to them (Simon and his brother Andrew), 'Follow me and I will make you fishers of people'" (Mk 1:17).

He is calling you to true discipleship. Christ is looking for those who will diligently seek Him. He calls us to be obedient, missional, humble, disciplined, and faithful children of His Father. Christ came to be an example and to teach us how to be disciples while empowering us to do more wondrous works than Him. The best reflection in all of the gospel accounts is not Christ but His faithful disciples because of His unique role in God's grand plan of salvation. It is Jesus's plan that we lead newly converted Christians into discipleship.

To clarify, a disciple is not just another new convert or a regular student. This is because a regular student will graduate at some time. Discipleship is not just something that can be completed after years of apprenticeship. Theologian Christopher Beard explains that the process of discipleship, although never really complete while the disciple remains on Earth, is nonetheless progressive.[6] The regeneration and transformation of a disciple is an ongoing process of the Holy Spirit working in our lives as we continue to live. In Him, we see the essential characteristics of true discipleship. This was why Christ said anyone who desires to be His disciple must first deny themselves, take up their cross daily, and follow Him (Lk 9:23).

Christ had twelve prominent disciples: Peter, Simon Zealots, James, John, Matthew, Andrew, Judas Thaddeus, Phillip, Thomas, Bartholomew, and Judas Iscariot, who betrayed Jesus. We are also aware of Christ's other seventy disciples aside from this inner circle. We learn from John that the seventy disciples stopped following Jesus after He told them and the crowd that they must drink His blood and eat His body for them to have eternal life (Jn 6:53, 66). However, His prominent twelve disciples stuck to Him and never left Him—apart from Judas, the betrayer. When Jesus asked if the twelve would also stop following Him, Peter, the disciples' spokesman, said, "Lord, to whom shall we go? Only you have the words that produce eternal life. He went further to say we believe and are sure that You are Christ, the Holy One of God" (Jn 6:68–69).

During the time of Christ, many people followed Him to listen to His preaching about God's kingdom. However, not all of them were His disciples. Some followed for their own reasons. Today, many people also follow Jesus for various reasons. Some follow to deceive, hoping to trap Him, while others seek healing, deliverance from demons, or to witness miracles. Some follow to receive prosperity, a better life, favor, or to claim the blessings promised to Abraham. Sadly, many people who follow Jesus today have hearts far from Him.

For disciples to be faithful followers of Christ, they must lose their lives for the kingdom's sake. There can be no greater glory than losing your life to follow Christ. This is what Jesus was trying to convey to the disciples. When Jesus told them in Matthew 16:24–26 to deny themselves by losing their lives for His sake, the disciples were all living in fear of death. However, after Jesus's death, resurrection, and the impartation of the Holy Spirit on the day of Pentecost, they were empowered and encouraged to lose their lives for the sake of the cross. To lose your life for Christ is to gain; this is what the world cannot understand.

Following Christ must mean everything to us; not even death can rob us of this glory. Christ repeatedly said that anyone who desires to save their life will lose it, and anyone who loses their life for Christ's sake will find it. The question before you right now is, "What will be your profit if you gain the whole world but lose your soul? Alternatively, what benefit will you receive in return for your soul" (Mt 16:25–26)?

Let us take a closer look at Luke 9:23, which is a critical text. In this passage, Jesus outlines four essential elements of being a disciple: desire, denial, carrying, and following. Regardless of your title, status, gender, race, ethnicity, denomination, or self-proclaimed spirituality, if you cannot fulfill these four elements, you cannot be considered a Christian or a true and faithful disciple of Christ. So, now that we understand what discipleship means, let us delve deeper into these critical elements.

Notes

[1] Sheldrake, Philip, *A Brief History of Spirituality* (Hoboken, NJ: Wiley, 2007), 24.

[2] Ibid, 24).

[3] Ibid.

[4] Ibid, 25.

[5] Ibid, 25.

[6]Christopher Beard, "Missional Discipleship: Discerning Spiritual-Formation Practices and Goals Within the Missional Movement," *Missiology* 43, no. 2 (Apr 2015): 175–94.

For Reflection

1. What does discipleship mean to you? What role has it played in your personal growth and development?

2. How does your understanding of discipleship influence your daily life and decision-making process?

3. How does discipleship contribute to your personal growth and development?

4. In what ways can you be a better disciple?

Food For Thought

The first step to true discipleship is that burning desire, which ignites and flames the whole process; without it, no one can truly and faithfully follow.

Two

THE CRITICAL ELEMENTS OF GENUINE FOLLOWERSHIP

If you desire to be a disciple, you must first deny yourself, take up your cross daily, and follow Him.[1]

Luke 9:23

Having a mindset that always seeks God's glory and follows the Lord's leading in everything helps me deny myself as I take up my cross daily. The Christian life is challenging, full of disciplining, and yielding control to the Holy Spirit. True Christianity is challenging because of our human nature, which is wired to be self-centered to avoid pain. Christ did not promise any of His followers a wonderful and cozy life, nor did He promise us a life without challenges. Instead, He said we would face many trials and tribulations for His sake. But through these difficulties, we will learn to find comfort in the uncomfortable, satisfaction even in little things, and peace in a troubled world. And if we remain steadfast until the end, He has promised us eternal life and the countless blessings that come with it.

As Jesus taught the crowd in Luke 9:23, Mark 8:34, and Matthew 16:24, to follow Jesus, we must put our own needs aside, carry our cross daily, and commit to His teachings. These words remind us that following His example requires daily sacrifice and devotion to His message. These sacrifices signify the cross we are called to carry as we live for the sake of God's kingdom. The cross represents the death of all that we hold dear. It is a chosen suffering, and no decision could be more bitter. It means dying to ourselves, for Christ's sake.

Although it may sound simple, those who cannot deny themselves and take up their cross daily are not living according to God's standards. These verses are critical to faithful followership and understanding how Christ sees His followers. They highlight the heart of Jesus's teachings to His disciples and emphasize the importance of following Him with devotion. They encourage us to embrace a selfless mindset, endure trials, and pursue a life dedicated to Christ. These verses speak to the transformative nature of following and the rewards of having a genuine relationship with Jesus. In His call for discipleship, Jesus emphasizes the critical aspects of genuine followership. Let us discuss each of them.

If You Desire

The decision to follow Christ is a profoundly personal experience. It often arises from a combination of faith, spiritual yearning, personal experiences, and a genuine desire for a relationship with God. Christ welcomes anyone who desires to be His disciple. However, following Christ is a process; initiating this must come from your heart. One must want or desire it genuinely, or else it will never happen. Even if it starts, it will fade quickly. Your desire to follow Christ must be more potent than any excuses you may have. This desire cannot be forced or merely wished for. Due to the sacrifices involved in following Christ, only those with a genuine and persistent desire for Christ can follow Him until the end. This is why it is essential to help those who are drifting away from the faith or losing trust in Christ to rekindle the burning desire that initiated their Christian journey. But how do most followers generate the desire to follow Christ?

The desire to follow Christ can arise from various motivations, inspirations, inclinations, and experiences. After years of study and experience, I have learned that there are noteworthy reasons why people may desire to follow Christ. Many of Christ's followers are inspired by their faith, belief, or deep conviction that Christ is the Messiah. Although they may not fully understand the source or depth of this inspiration, it gives them a firm conviction that Christ is the Son of God who has come to save them. They have faith in His teachings, His life, His sacrificial love, His death, His resurrection, and the hope of eternal life He presents to them. Other people desire to follow Christ because they crave spiritual fulfillment and a sense of purpose that produces meaningful and productive life.

The darkness and emptiness of this world can create a spiritual yearning that draws people closer to the feet of Jesus. This craving may arise from the book of Hebrews, which encourages us to confidently approach God's throne of grace to obtain mercy and find grace to help us in our times of need. These people believe that only by following Jesus can they receive the guidance, connection to God, and meaning they seek. Meanwhile, others may be motivated by the promise of personal transformation that ushers us to the promised eternal life. Christ's message also offers spiritual formation and inner peace that transcends human understanding. It draws those who desire positive change with teachings on forgiveness, love, and compassion.

The desire to follow Christ may also arise from observing His impact on others and experiencing the power of His love firsthand. For example, when those around you see Christ's transformative power at work in your life, it can inspire them to follow Him. It can be compelling to follow Christ when your life reflects Christ to the point that those around you witness the love and positive transformations you demonstrate. Burning desires also emerge from those who are earnestly searching for truth. Such desires surface from those who embark on a journey of discovery to seek truth, knowledge, perspicuity, and explanations to life's most profound questions.

Jesus proclaimed that He is the only way, the truth, and the life. Once truth seekers encounter Jesus, they quickly realize His teachings and wisdom offer profound insights and the perfect framework for their spiritual journey. The desire to follow Christ is a unique and deeply personal experience. When you are evangelizing for Christ, it is crucial to understand how the desire to follow Christ arises. The desire for discipleship often stems from faith and belief, spiritual passion, personal experiences, and a genuine longing for a relationship with God.

Deny Yourself

To serve and follow God, you must first deny yourself. Denying yourself means relinquishing selfish desires, priorities, and ego and surrendering your will to place God's will above all else. Doing so empowers you to prioritize what is essential in life and follow God's path. The word "deny" comes from the Greek root word *aparneomai,* which means to assert that one has no connection or acquaintance with a person, place, or thing. It also means forgetting yourself and losing sight of yourself and your interests. Denying yourself or your old ways for Christ's sake involves a conscious decision to prioritize Christ's will and the kingdom's principles over your desires, self-centeredness, and ambitions. It doesn't mean that we should not enjoy the blessings and comfort that God has given us. Unlike some strict religious or extreme spiritual disciplines, it doesn't require us to live like monks or other religious sects who impose extreme control on their members' actions. It is more about disciplining yourself per the Holy Scriptures.

Disciplining yourself involves surrendering to the Holy Spirit's guidance until it becomes a habit. Denying yourself means rejecting the things that may obstruct your path toward God's kingdom, such as money, fame, power, rights, privileges, and comforts. However, what we must deny may vary depending on our desires, situation, and relationships with God and others. It could be societal expectations, pleasures, comforts, or responsibilities for one another. It could be relational or personal baggage. As you discipline yourself, your desires should align with God's values, which may differ from those of the world or unbelievers. If you realize your desires and values still align with secular values, it should give you cause for self-examination.

Following Christ requires us to reject the societal norms contradicting the Bible's teachings. We cannot claim to be faithful Christians while practicing shallow, selfish, and sinful behavior or by trying to please society with a watered-down version of our faith. Such behavior is hypocritical and can lead to spiritual destruction. Faithful followers of Christ should be willing to surrender their entire being to His will, including their words, attitudes, and actions. Holding on to our selfish desires or making excuses is self-deception, not faith. Denying ourselves of these excuses is a significant step toward following Christ.

One day, as Jesus and His disciples walked along the road, a man approached and declared that he would be willing to follow Jesus wherever He went. With a gentle smile, Jesus said that even though foxes have cozy dens and birds have warm nests, the Son of Man (referring to Himself) has no place to call home. His words were spoken with a hint of sadness, revealing the sacrifice He had made to spread His message of love and salvation to all who would listen. In other words, following Jesus would be a challenging journey. Jesus was asking His followers if they were ready to rough it with Him, as they would have to deny themselves a lot of things, and they would not be able to stay in the best inns. Then Jesus asked another person to follow Him. The person's response was shocking, as he said he would follow Jesus, but first, he needed to excuse himself for a few days to plan his father's funeral. Jesus reminded the man that his business is life, not death, and that proclaiming God's kingdom should be his utmost priority.

Yet another person said to Jesus, "Lord, I will follow you, but first, let me go back and take care of family business or straighten out things at home." Jesus used metaphorical language to make a point about commitment. He said that anyone who begins plowing a field and then looks back is not suited for serving in God's kingdom. This implies that those who start something but get distracted or lose focus will not succeed in their spiritual journey. Once you have decided to follow Christ, there is no room for procrastination or backward looks. You cannot put off God's kingdom till tomorrow. Seek first God's kingdom, seize the day, deny yourself, pick up your cross, and follow Christ. These are the costs of following Jesus (Lk 9:57–62).

How Can You Deny Yourself for the Sake of Christ?

Earlier, we discussed the concept of denying yourself, which involves prioritizing Christ's will and kingdom principles over yourself. It requires letting go of your desires, self-centeredness, and ambitions. There are various ways to strip yourself of the old ways to follow Christ. One of the most well-known passages in the Apostle Paul's letters to the Corinthians addresses this issue. He says, "Therefore, if you are in Christ, the new creation—the Christ-given life—has come: The old—yourself that you need to deny—has gone, your new life in Christ is here!" (2 Cor 5:17). Let's delve into some of these practices, which can help if you're struggling with denying your old ways.

The first step is to surrender your will to the cross. You must surrender all your desires, ambitions, and plans to God's will. Instead of pursuing personal gratification or selfish goals, you must align your life with God's will, desires, and plans. Seek His guidance and be prepared to obey His commandments—endeavor to always love as He has commanded.

Denying yourself to follow Christ is also a call to the continuous act of sacrificial love. Sacrificial love is self-sacrifice that emanates from the pure motivation to positively impact others or alleviate their despair. However, Christ has repeatedly called us to love even our enemies. He commands all His followers to love others daily with sacrificial love. This love should always manifest itself in action, creating a positive and lasting impression that inspires others to follow.

The Bible tells us that God loves us unconditionally and demonstrated this love by sending His Son to die for us while we were still sinners (Rom 5:8). From the beginning, Jesus showed us His endless love without any conditions. He loves us not because of our looks or because we show interest in Him but simply because of who we are—His children. Christ has taught us to love others sacrificially, as He demonstrated through His life, death, and teachings. This means showing compassion and forgiveness and putting the needs of others before our own. It requires serving those around us selflessly. To reach this level of serving God and others, we must discipline ourselves to crucify our sinful desires. The Apostle Paul taught that to belong to Christ, we must nail the passions and desires of our sinful nature to the cross (Gal 5:24).

You must also crucify the sinful desires of the flesh as an act of denying yourself to follow Christ. We must crucify all connections to our selfish ways and how we respond to necessities. Self-denial includes saying no to sinful temptations. It is persevering to live a life that mirrors Christ's righteousness. One sure thing is that every day, you will be tempted. You will never be too old, mature, or holy for it. As long as you are alive, you will be tempted. Scripture reminds us, "No temptation has seized you except what is common to man" (1 Cor 10:13). We all have our fair share of struggles and temptations, but through Christ's amazing and saving grace, we can triumph over all our trials and temptations with joy. One interesting fact about temptation is that it is not just the elephant in the room; it can also come as the tiniest insect, making it difficult to see.

Temptation can take many forms, often starting with a simple thought. It might begin with the temptation to lie to escape trouble or the thought of cheating on a spouse, evading taxes, or not speaking up when you notice a mistake in your favor. Temptations may also come in the form of seeking quick satisfaction by holding onto grudges, refusing to let go, or wishing ill on your enemies. It can even present itself as a desire to lie, falsify records, or disobey authority.

Temptations themselves are not sinful. However, indulging them leads to sin. We often downplay "little sins" as harmless, but these sins pave the way for the enemy to steal, kill, and destroy, leading to spiritual death. To follow Christ, we must deny ourselves and overcome our sinful tendencies, striving for righteousness and allowing the Holy Spirit to transform us from within. Denying yourself also requires being humble and serving others with compassion and kindness.

Christ was a living example of humility and servanthood, exemplifying these traits throughout His life. To embody humility, we must reject our pride and ego and acknowledge that we are not the center of the universe. Instead, we should seek opportunities to serve and uplift others. These characteristics are essential for any disciple, and this book explores them in depth. As disciples, we must also practice self-denial by distancing ourselves from material and worldly pursuits. These things can quickly become distractions and idols that hinder our faithfulness to Christ. By simplifying our lives and finding contentment in our blessings, we can use our resources to support others and increase our devotion to Christ.

An Important Note

Self-denial is not about self-deprecation or punishing yourself. Instead, it is the act of redirecting your focus and priorities toward God's kingdom. When we make God our priority, it has a positive impact on everyone around us. In the Sermon on the Mount, Christ encourages us to seek God's kingdom and its demands above all else. When we do so, He promises to provide us with all our needs (Mt 6:33). God does this by bringing gifts into our lives, just like fruit appears in an orchard. When we prioritize God's kingdom, we experience growth in the fruit of the spirit, love for others, a joyful life, and peace. Prioritizing God also leads to a willingness to obey, a compassionate heart, and a renewed spirit. It helps us understand that holiness is present in all things and all people. Although self-denial may seem challenging, communicating with God through prayer, studying the Holy Scriptures, and seeking the Holy Spirit's guidance will help us through the process. By praying, learning, and seeking God's guidance, we draw closer to the throne of grace, where we find help. The book of Hebrews tells us to come boldly to the throne of our compassionate God, where we receive His mercy and find grace to help us overcome our desires, deny our flesh, and carry our cross as we follow Him (Heb 4:16).

Carry Your Cross Daily

The cross is the ultimate symbol of hope, salvation, transfiguration, unending joy, and eternal life. It also represents the hardships, challenges, and sacrifices that come with following Jesus. It reminds us that being a disciple involves difficulties but ultimately leads to spiritual growth and eternal life. Taking up your cross daily does not equate to being under a specific burden from God or the Church. It is equivalent to denying [your]self in implication. If we learn to sacrifice ourselves to God, we will not fret about sacrificing our things. We will belong to God, not our material things, position, power, reputation, or comfort. Luke 9:23 mentions taking up your cross daily, which means embracing the challenges and sacrifices of following Christ. We can live out this principle by finding practical ways to take up our cross daily.

Becoming a disciple of Christ requires you to adopt the principle of unwavering commitment to following Him. It also requires dedication to His teachings, serving His people, and persevering through difficulties and opposition. The stronger your commitment to Christ, the more you can triumph over life's challenges. To deepen your commitment to Christ, you must surrender control to Him and trust His guidance. This requires steadfastness, perseverance, and an unwavering trust in God's faithfulness. Surrendering control to Christ means recognizing that God's plans may not always align with your desires, expectations, or plans. It means trusting Him even when it makes no sense or leads you on a path that you would not have chosen for yourself. To surrender control to Christ, you must trust His wisdom and accept His guidance. This means trusting Him even when it seems like your world is falling apart. You must let go of your desires and plans as you trust that God knows what is best for you.

As followers of Christ, our trust in Him enables us to endure difficulties and trials that surpass human understanding. Trials are a natural part of the Christian life, so it is crucial to have a strong desire to follow Christ. In his epistle, James encourages us to be joyful in the face of any trial, recognizing it as an opportunity for tremendous satisfaction in Christ. When our faith is tested, it provides an excellent opportunity to grow, leading us to become fitting, perfect, and complete, lacking nothing (Jas 1:2–4). Through James's message, we learn that trials and difficulties are not just obstacles to overcome; they can also lead to spiritual growth and refinement.

When facing trials, we must rely on God's wisdom and strength to navigate them. In doing so, we develop a deeper understanding of God and what He can do in our lives. We discover that trials can be opportunities for spiritual formation as we learn to trust God more. Following Jesus means embracing difficulties and seeking God's wisdom and strength to navigate them. When we do this, we become more like Christ and discover the fullness of His love and grace. Therefore, every trial and difficulty we encounter is a chance to grow in our faith, deepen our relationship with God, and become more like the people Jesus has called us to be.

Living out the principle of taking up your cross is a practical way to show devotion. As mentioned earlier, self-denial is a daily practice that involves putting God's needs first, followed by the needs of others before our own. In most cases, God's needs are reflected in the needs of those around us. Practicing self-denial may mean sacrificing our comfort, desires, and preferences to serve God and loving others sacrificially. Taking up your cross daily requires courage, determination, boldness, and a firm belief in God.

For this reason, disciples must be willing to stand up for righteousness, truth, and justice, even in times of abundance, in the face of opposition and persecution. Taking up your cross daily means that it is no longer your will that should be done but God's. A life dependent on Christ must seek God's will in everything. This requires us to look at the world, everyone, and everything through God's will. To know God's will, it is essential to seek His guidance regularly. We can ask Him to reveal His heart to us through prayer and studying His Word, which can lead to spending time in His presence. If you want to know God's purpose for your life, you must ask Him to reveal it. As the Holy Scriptures say, "Everyone who asks receives, and those who seek will find what they are looking for" (Mt 7:7–8). Keep an open mind and heart to His leading, even if it challenges your comfort zone. Taking up your cross is also about aligning your words, thoughts, actions, attitudes, and decisions with Jesus's principles. Living a life that honors and venerates Him means taking up your cross. Doing this daily means continually following Jesus and embracing His way of life, death, and resurrection. Rely on His strength and seek His guidance to walk the path of genuine and committed followership.

And Follow Me

To follow Jesus means to commit to living out His teachings, lifestyle, and example. This involves walking in His footsteps, adopting His values, and spreading His message of love and redemption. God's ultimate plan is to bring all people to Him, and this includes mobilizing an army, the Body of Christ, through discipleship to glorify Him while destroying the enemy's work. Faithfully following

Christ is the only way to glorify God and possess the power and authority to destroy the enemy's works. As Christians, everything we do should revolve around following Christ from the moment we confess Him as our Lord and Savior. The author of Hebrews urges us to focus on Christ, the Savior, who is the author and perfecter of our faith. He endured the cross, disregarding its shame, and sat down at the right hand of God's throne for the joy set before Him. Let us focus on Jesus, who stood firm in the face of intense hostility from sinners. By looking to Him, we can find the strength to persevere and avoid growing tired or discouraged. These words of encouragement can be found in Hebrews 12:2–3.

We can say that we walk according to God's plan when we carry our cross and follow Him daily. Gradually, we will grow as disciples of Christ. As part of our followership, we learn the ways of Christ, emulate them, and teach them to others. This is what discipleship is all about. God's way of bringing all people to glorify Him is through discipleship, as portrayed in the famous Great Commission in Matthew 28:16–20.

At the core of discipleship lies the individual. Each of us has a role in spreading Christ's message to the world. Through our personal transformation, the impact of Christ's message begins to extend to those around us. The Body of Christ has been given all power in heaven and on earth to handle any problem and provide for all needs. But to unleash this power, we must understand our identity in Christ, calling, purpose, position, and endowments.

Pursuing Christ and His presence is the key to unlocking the power of the Body of Christ. It is through this pursuit that we become more like Him. This is a challenging journey, requiring us to surrender our will and our desires to Him. We must be willing to yield our minds and hearts to Him, see things the way He sees them, hear things the way He hears them, and speak as He speaks. The question is, are we willing and able? Are we pursuing the Lord,

His presence, and the suffering that comes with obeying His will, or are we seeking only the benefits? Are we seeking to be like Him? As He created us in His image, are we seeking to yield our minds and hearts to Him? As urged by the Apostle Paul in Romans 12, are we ready to offer ourselves as a living sacrifice, refrain from the pattern of this world, and let the Holy Spirit renew our minds?

I think answering these questions requires a thorough self-examination. We must be willing to be broken like clay in the Potter's hand, allowing God to mold us into the image of His Son. Only then can we experience true satisfaction in Christ. Through this transformation, we can extend love, compassion, and grace to those around us, enabling them to see the Christ in us. Today's world desperately needs love, power, forgiveness, understanding, and acceptance. As disciples of Christ, we are called to embody these virtues. The first step toward fulfilling this calling is to have a flaming desire to follow Christ. This desire must burn within us, producing a willingness to be available for the Potter to mold us to His will as we carry our cross and follow Him daily. Only then can we become the salt and light of the world, fulfilling God's purposes for our lives. Please do not forget, nor let anyone deceive you; everything we need in our Christian journey is contained in the Holy Bible.

Note

[1] Also, in Mark 8:34 and Matthew 16:24.

For Reflection

1. Do you agree with the author that living a Christian life is challenging? What are your thoughts on this matter?

2. What inspired you to follow Christ? Can you reflect on the motivations, inspirations, inclinations, or experiences that led you to Him?

3. How do you balance the desire to follow Christ with the need to maintain your own autonomy and individuality?

4. How will you integrate discipleship principles and your new knowledge of discipleship into your daily life and relationships?

5. What practical steps can you take to deepen your understanding and the practice of discipleship?

Food for Thought

Resisting the world's temptations is a testament to your unwavering strength and steadfast conviction. When you stay true to your beliefs and do not bow to societal pressures, you will unlock the door to your inner peace and a deeper connection with God.

Three

THE LEADING
TEMPTATIONS OF A
DISCIPLE

> *Our desires are the source of temptation. They lure us and lead us astray.*
>
> **James 1:14**

We are unique beings that embody the spirit, body, and soul and are endowed with the gift of free will. These characteristics expose us to inner conflicts that arise from our desires. These desires can be compelling, luring us toward them even when we know deep down that they are not in our best interest. This struggle between what we want and what we know is right can be overwhelming, but it is also an opportunity for growth and transformation. This chapter calls to embrace a profoundly cross-centered idea of discipleship with proper knowledge of the leading temptations facing Christians. It also reminds us that temptations do not come from God but from within ourselves.

It may be surprising to learn that Satan, whom we often blame for our temptations, is not the culprit, as we must learn to take responsibility for our actions and decisions. Let us set aside our self-denial and pay attention to what James, the half-brother of Jesus, says about temptation. Understanding how temptations come from within us helps us navigate the challenges and pitfalls that threaten to pull us away from following Christ. This is a challenging journey, but it is well worth taking. We can overcome our inner conflicts and become the best versions of ourselves with commitment and dedication.

In the first chapter of James, he employs a captivating fishing illustration to explain the intricacies of temptation and how it originates from within us. James emphasizes that our desires entice us. This is similar to a fisherman placing bait on a hook and dangling it before a fish. The author points out that if we have no desires that Satan could exploit, he would have nothing to tempt us with. Satan is like a fisherman. With calculated movements, he secures the bait onto the hook and casts the line into the water with a flick of his wrist. The surface ripples as the bait sinks deeper into the unknown depths, but the true temptation does not lie in the shimmering bait. Instead, it stirs within us a burning desire to capture the elusive catch. Brother James says temptation only becomes compelling and intense based on our desires. Just as a fish may not be interested in an orange on the hook, Satan cannot tempt us if we do not desire what he offers. James says the problem lies within us, not with God, who does not tempt us. It lies in how we respond to our desires. We must resist Satan's ways and find holy and godly methods of fulfilling our heart desires. Let us take the first biblical account of temptation as an example.

In the Garden of Eden, Eve was enticed by the snake to consume the fruit that God prohibited. The serpent questioned the commandment that prohibited Eve and Adam from consuming the fruit of the tree of the knowledge of good and evil. With persuasive words, the serpent convinced Eve that by eating the fruit, she would not die but instead become like God, possessing knowledge and wisdom beyond what God granted her. The serpent's words sparked an intense desire within Eve to gain knowledge, which led her to succumb to temptation. She picked the fruit and ate it, and then, without hesitation, she offered some to Adam, who also ate it. This act of disobedience caused the fall of humanity and led to their expulsion from the Garden of Eden.

James highlights that our struggle with sin and temptation stems from our desires. Therefore, we must acknowledge our weaknesses and understand our desires to overcome them. Eve's desire was not to die but to become like God and possess knowledge and wisdom beyond what God had established for her and Adam. In the same way, we need to identify the things that can lure us away, as James describes in his illustration.

Four great temptations have affected Christians, especially our Christian leaders today, to a dangerous extent: the desire for money, relevance, fame, and power. Most consider these four elements of a fruitful ministry, but I treat them as leading temptations that can easily trip us during our heavenly race.

The temptation of money, power, fame, and relevance-seeking behavior can intertwine and pose significant challenges to Christian beliefs and values. They all offer a sense of control, status, and recognition, often conflicting with the teachings of humility, service, and prioritizing spiritual values. Money tempts individuals with material wealth, offering comfort and security. Pursuing wealth can overshadow the importance of faith, generosity, and stewardship. Power offers control and influence. It can lead to self-centered decisions, overriding the teachings of servant leadership and self-lessness taught in Christianity. Fame provides recognition and admiration. The desire for fame may foster a self-centered focus, contradicting the humility and modesty advocated in Christian teachings.

Relevance-seeking behavior can sometimes compromise your core values in favor of societal approval, diluting your commitment to spiritual principles. The common thread among these temptations is their potential to draw your attention away from the core teachings of Christianity, such as humility, service, and faithfulness. Indulging these temptations encourages focusing on the self rather than selfless service, humility, and adherence to Christian values. Balancing these desires with the teachings of faith, service, and humility becomes a challenge for Christians when navigating their everyday lives. Let us get a more profound understanding of these temptations.

The Desire for Wealth

> *The endless pursuit of wealth has been known to bring about various forms of evil, leaving one feeling hollow and unfulfilled.*
> **1 Timothy 6:10**

Usually, the first temptation Christians face is the desire for wealth. Money is one of the leading temptations in Christian discipleship due to its ability to become a primary focus or an object of worship, taking precedence over spiritual values. Its allure can lead to greed, materialism, and avarice, pulling individuals away from their spiritual path. The Bible often warns about the potential dangers of loving money more than God, emphasizing the importance of placing spiritual values over material wealth. The temptation lies in the power money holds to influence choices, values, and priorities, often leading individuals away from the teachings of humility, generosity, and selflessness. Pursuing wealth and material possessions has long been identified as a significant source of various evils. Those who chase after money with a single-minded focus are often led astray from what truly matters. In their quest for financial gain, they lose sight of their values and beliefs, causing them to become embroiled in situations that bring nothing but pain and misery. It is a tragic reality that many people have been consumed by the desire for wealth, only to find themselves lost and alone in a sea of troubles.

The temptation of wealth has caused many Christians to idolize money due to its perceived power to provide security, comfort, and status. In a world where financial success is often equated with achievement and happiness, the pursuit of money can overshadow spiritual values. Moreover, consumer culture and societal pressures usually reinforce the idea that wealth equals success and fulfillment. This emphasis can lead to the prioritization of financial gain over humility, generosity, and spiritual well-being, gradually turning money into an idol that takes precedence over faith. The allure of material possessions and the promise of a comfortable life can overshadow the spiritual principles taught within Christianity, leading to the idolization of money, harmful outcomes, and loss of faith in ourselves and others. Ultimately, it leads people to sorrow and despair. As we continue to discuss the lustful desire for wealth, let me share some scriptural guidance on money.

Biblical Guidance on Money

Prioritize God Over Money

In Matthew 6:24, Jesus teaches that serving God and money is impossible. Therefore, as Christians, we are called to prioritize our relationship with God over pursuing wealth. This means our faith and biblical teachings should guide our actions, decisions, and ambitions. In this way, we acknowledge that our ultimate source of security and fulfillment is not material possessions but our identity in Christ. This does not mean we cannot work hard or enjoy the blessings that come with financial prosperity, but rather that we should not allow money to become an idol or a substitute for our devotion to God.

Practice Contentment

In Philippians 4:11–12, the Apostle Paul encourages the practice of contentment regardless of financial circumstances. This means we must cultivate a state of mind that is satisfied with what we have and not focus excessively on accumulating wealth. Such an attitude fosters an appreciation of our blessings and reduces our desire for more. By practicing contentment, we can find joy and peace in our present situation rather than constantly chasing after the elusive promise of wealth and success.

Generosity and Giving

In Acts 20:35, the Apostle Paul reminds us of the joy that comes from giving to others rather than receiving. This passage highlights the importance of generosity and selflessness. By shifting our focus away from personal wealth and toward the well-being of those around us, we experience a more profound sense of purpose and fulfillment. When we freely give our time, resources, and talents, we help others and cultivate gratitude and humility. In this way, generosity and giving become a source of joy and blessing for the giver and the receiver.

Stewardship

The parable of the talents, as narrated in Matthew 25:14–30, is a powerful lesson on the importance of responsible stewardship of resources, especially money. The story tells of a master who went on a trip and commissioned his belongings to his servants, giving one five talents, another two talents, and another one talent, according to their respective abilities. The first two servants invested and doubled their talents, while the third buried his talent out of fear and did not increase it. The master returned and praised the first two servants, saying, "You have done well, my good and faithful servants! You have been trustworthy with the little I gave you. So, I will put you in charge of many things. Come and share your master's happiness!" However, he scolded the third servant, calling him wicked and lazy, and took away his talent, giving it to the one with ten talents.

This parable teaches that we are all stewards of the resources God has given us and will be held accountable for how we use them. Therefore, Christians are encouraged to acknowledge money as a gift from God and should be utilized to benefit others and advance God's Kingdom. By doing so, we will be faithful and fruitful stewards and will be rewarded by our Master when He returns.

Seek the Kingdom of God

Matthew 6:33 is a powerful reminder from Jesus to prioritize seeking the Kingdom of God above all else. This means putting God's will and the pursuit of righteousness at the center of your life and trusting that all other needs will be taken care of. Seeking God's kingdom requires a heart open to God's guidance and willing to surrender to His will. It is a journey of faith and devotion that brings joy, peace, and fulfillment.

When we seek God's kingdom, we are not focused on material wealth or temporal pleasures. Instead, we pursue a higher purpose and a deeper relationship with God. We are committed to spiritual growth and alignment with God's will, which leads to a life rich in meaning and purpose. Seeking God's kingdom requires us to prioritize our relationship with God above all else. It also means we acknowledge that our security and provision come from God. We can trust that He will provide for our needs both materially and spiritually as we seek to honor Him with our lives. This gives us a sense of freedom and peace that cannot be found in any earthly pursuit.

Community and Accountability

Being part of a faith community is incredibly valuable for individuals seeking support and personal growth. Proverbs 27:17 emphasizes the significance of mutual support, using the image of iron sharpening iron. When Christians apply these teachings in their lives, they can redirect their attention from the worship of money to the practice of faith, gratitude, generosity, and responsible stewardship. You can formulate a sense of meaning and purpose via your faith community when you stay grounded and accountable for your priorities.

In Christian discipleship, money should be viewed as a reflection of your heart and priorities. It should be seen as a tool rather than an end in itself. The emphasis is on using money responsibly, being generous, and sharing resources to help others. It's not just about giving but also about our attitude toward wealth, acknowledging that everything belongs to God. The Bible's teachings regarding money emphasize stewardship, encouraging individuals to manage money wisely, support charitable causes, and align their financial choices with their values and faith principles.

Practical Ways to Overcome the Temptation of Pursuing Wealth

View Yourself as a Steward

One practical approach is cultivating a stewardship mindset, acknowledging that all wealth belongs to God and that we are entrusted to manage it wisely. Setting clear priorities, such as giving generously and living within your means, will help you maintain your focus on spiritual values over material wealth. Regular self-reflection, prayer, and seeking accountability through a community can also help keep your focus on faith rather than money. Additionally, engaging in acts of service and generosity can help redirect our focus away from personal wealth and toward contributing to the well-being of others.

Create a Balanced Budget

Creating a balanced budget that aligns with Christian principles requires considering several factors. First, it's crucial to prioritize necessities such as housing, food, and health care. As the Apostle Paul urges in 1 Timothy 6:8, "True godliness with contentment is itself great wealth. After all, we brought nothing with us when we came into the world, and we can't take anything with us when we leave it. So, if we have enough food and clothing, let us be content." Let us embrace the Apostle Paul's wisdom and find contentment in life's simple blessings. This ensures that we can maintain a basic standard of living.

Second, allocate a portion of your budget toward savings. Proverbs 21:20 reminds us of the importance of wise decisions in every area of our lives. The verse encourages us to store choice food and olive oil, symbolizing the value of investing in high-quality resources that will sustain us in times of need.

On the other hand, the verse warns us against being foolish and hastily consuming our resources, which can lead to scarcity and hardship. This could include setting aside funds for emergencies or long-term goals such as purchasing a home, paying for education, or retirement. May we all strive to be wise in our decisions so we may live abundant and fulfilling lives.

Your budget should also prioritize generosity toward others. Luke 6:38 encourages us to be generous and give freely. It reminds us that giving benefits others and rewards us in return. Therefore, strive to be gracious in your giving. Money should be used to help those in need. This can involve charitable donations, tithing, or other forms of giving back to the community.

By emphasizing generosity toward others, you can live out the principles of Christian stewardship. A balanced budget that considers these principles can help you handle your finances responsibly and sustainably. Proverbs 22:7 states that the rich rule over the poor and that the borrower is a slave to the lender. By heeding these principles, you can detour around financial hurdles and use your resources to serve God.

Reflect Regularly on Your Values

Reflecting on your values and principles is a crucial biblical concept to ensure that our financial decisions align with our beliefs. Proverbs 3:6 holds excellent wisdom: "If you acknowledge the Lord in all your ways, he will make your paths straight." This means you can count on God to direct you down the right path by putting your faith in the Lord and following His guidance. This practice helps us clarify what matters most and make intentional choices that align with our core values. Matthew 6:21 reminds us that our hearts are often tied to our material possessions. When we invest our time, energy, and resources into things that matter, we cultivate a sense of purpose and fulfillment that cannot be found in material wealth alone. So, strive to focus on the treasures of the heart, knowing that they accurately measure our wealth and happiness.

We can lead more fulfilling and intentional lives by aligning our monetary decisions with our values. First, Timothy 6:10 highlights the negative consequences of an unhealthy attachment to wealth. This verse suggests that the love of money can usher people down a pathway of moral corruption and cause them to stray from their beliefs. As a result of this craving for riches, some may inflict pain upon themselves and others, causing harm to their physical, emotional, and spiritual well-being. Reflecting on our values and ensuring that our financial decisions are aligned with them is crucial for leading a virtuous and fulfilling life.

Practice Gratitude

Practicing gratitude is an essential aspect of our daily lives as Christians. It is an assertive emotion that can significantly impact our well-being. As the apostle Paul says in 1 Thessalonians 5:18, "Show appreciation in all situations; for it is God's will for you." By developing a heart of gratitude, we can appreciate what we have and feel content with our present circumstances. As Christians, we should be grateful for the people in our lives, the opportunities we've been given, and our possessions. Philippians 4:6–7 reminds us that we don't have to be anxious no matter what we're going through. All we need to do is pray with thanksgiving and present our requests to God. He promises to give us peace that exceeds human understanding and safeguard our hearts and minds in Christ Jesus.

Focusing on what we lack makes us feel stressed and unhappy. Redirecting our focus toward what we have will improve our mood, reduce stress, and strengthen our relationships. It will also help us see the world more positively and feel more satisfied with our current situation. In Colossians 3:15–17, Paul reminds us to allow the peace of Christ to rule in our hearts, as we are called to be peaceful members of one body. We should be grateful and express our gratitude through actions, words, and songs. Prioritize having Christ's message dwell within you so you can use it to teach and guide others. You can do this using psalms, hymns, and other Spirit-inspired songs.

As you sing to God with gratitude, remember to do everything in the name of the Lord Jesus and show your appreciation to God the Father through Him. Being grateful doesn't mean we can't strive for more, but it's paramount that we appreciate what we have already accomplished. In 2 Corinthians 9:11, Paul writes, "You will be enriched in all ways so you can be beneficial on every occasion, and through us, your benefaction will result in thanksgiving to God." Whether it's a good job, a loving relationship, or good health, we should be thankful for it.

Seek Accountability

To attain contentment and spiritual growth, it is vital to seek accountability and support from like-minded individuals, as stated in Proverbs 27:17, "As iron sharpens iron, so one person sharpens another." A community or an accountability partner who shares your values can motivate you to stay on track and make progress toward your goals, as expressed in the book of Ecclesiastes, "Two are better than one, for they can achieve more by working together. If one falls, the other can help them up. But it is unfortunate for anyone who falls and has no one to help them up" (Ecc 4:9–10). This support system can help you shift your focus from material-istic pursuits to more meaningful ones, leading to a more fulfilling and spiritually enriching life. As Matthew 6:19–21 warns, "Focus on building eternal treasures instead of temporary ones. Earthly possessions are fleeting and can be lost or stolen, but the treasures we accumulate in heaven are everlasting. By prioritizing what truly matters, we can live a fulfilling life with a lasting impact on the world around us."

Prioritize Giving

By prioritizing generosity over materialistic pursuits, you can positively impact the world around you while reaping personal benefits such as increased happiness and a sense of fulfillment. If you embrace giving as a core value, your financial choices will make a positive difference.

Avoid Excessive Materialism

In a society that values material possessions, we must be mindful of our consumption habits and limit our materialism. By doing so, we can prioritize our spiritual growth and shift our focus toward serving others. It's about finding balance and recognizing that fulfillment and happiness come from within rather than from the things we own. Taking this approach can lead to a more meaningful and fulfilling life, where we find joy in the simple things and derive satisfaction from positively impacting the world around us.

Engage in Regular Spiritual Practices

Regular spiritual practices are essential for building a robust connection with your inner self and the Almighty. Engaging in daily prayer, meditation, and other spiritual practices helps to ground you and develop a deeper understanding of the world around us. These practices can also reduce the influence of material wealth and encourage a more meaningful and fulfilling life focused on spiritual growth. Applying these steps consistently helps to reinforce the prioritization of spiritual values over the pursuit of wealth.

The Desire for Relevance

In today's world, the temptation to be relevant affects many Christians. It can be easy to get caught up in the desire to be popular, famous, or influential, but as followers of Christ, our focus should be on serving God and others. The desire to be relevant often drives us to strive for greatness, seek to prove ourselves, or prioritize impressing others over God's plan for our lives and ministry. This impulse can cause us to compromise our faith, dilute the gospel, and live a life that is more focused on secular success than following Christ. In his book, *In the Name of Jesus: Reflections on Christian Leadership,* noted professor and theologian Father Henri Nouwen suggests that future Christian leaders must learn to be wholly irrelevant and stand in this world with nothing to offer but their vulnerable selves.[1] This means giving up our desire to be relevant and instead embracing a deeper understanding of the pain and suffering in the world.

A question remains for us as believers: how much do we love Jesus, and how willing are we to empty ourselves for Him? To do so, we must discipline ourselves through holy desire, self-denial, and contemplative prayer, all of which help us to attain intimacy with God. These practices help us overcome the temptation to focus on relevance and instead remain focused on our relationship with Christ. We express our longing for God and our desire to know Him better through self-denial and holy desire. Self-denial is the practice of putting the needs of others before our own. This discipline helps us to become humbler and more compassionate toward others. On the other hand, holy desire requires contemplative prayer, deep reflection, and meditation on His truth. This practice helps us to connect with God.

By embracing these practices, we can overcome the temptation to focus on relevance and instead remain focused on our relationship with Christ. This allows us to follow His will for our lives and ministry, even if it means going against secular norms. Ultimately, we must remember that our goal as Christians is not to impress others but to follow Christ and bring glory to His name. Our worth and significance come from our relationship with God and not from the world's standards of success. Jesus was tempted in many ways during His time on Earth, including a temptation toward relevance. We can see this example when the devil tempted Jesus in the wilderness. Satan tempted Jesus to perform miracles to prove His power and relevance. However, Jesus resisted this temptation and instead focused on His mission to save humanity and follow God's will.

How to Overcome the Temptation Toward Relevance

Overcoming the temptation to be relevant involves shifting our focus from seeking worldly approval to prioritizing obedience to God and faithfulness to His teachings. Here are some steps to help in overcoming this temptation.

Seek God's Perspective

To live purposefully, seeking God's wisdom and guidance in prayer is essential. James 1:5–6 encourages us to seek wisdom by asking God. According to this passage, God is generous and gives wisdom without finding fault. However, it is paramount to believe and not doubt when we ask for wisdom, as doubting is like being adrift at sea, blown and tossed about by the wind. Ask God to help you align your deepest desires with His divine will and to give you the strength to resist the allure of relevance-seeking distractions that pull you away from the path He has laid for you. Jesus maintained a deep and intimate relationship with His Heavenly Father through prayer. He regularly sought God's guidance, strength, and wisdom. Prayer gave Jesus the spiritual fortitude to resist temptation and remain aligned with God's purposes.

Anchor Yourself in God's Word

To live a life guided by God's truth, it is crucial to delve deeply into Jesus's teachings and the principles laid out in the Bible. By studying and meditating on these foundational texts, you can gain a comprehensive understanding of God's truth and how it applies to your life. This understanding can shape your perspective and actions, leading you toward a life of purpose and fulfillment. Jesus countered each temptation with the truth of God's Word. He relied on Scripture as guidance, strength, and clarity. By anchoring Himself in God's revealed truth, Jesus remained steadfast in His commitment to God's will rather than seeking worldly relevance.

Prioritize Obedience

In a world where societal relevance, fame, and public acceptance are celebrated, we must prioritize obedience to God above all else. The path to true purpose and relevance can only be found by living according to God's will. This requires resisting the temptation to conform to societal expectations and instead following the unique path that God has set for each of us. By living according to God's will, we can lead fulfilling and meaningful lives that far exceed the temporary pleasures of worldly achievements. These accomplishments may bring us momentary happiness. However, they are fleeting and will never provide the lasting contentment of living a life aligned with God's plan.

Jesus's life provides us with a perfect example of the importance of prioritizing obedience to God. He understood that His ultimate purpose was to fulfill God's plan of salvation, which required Him to make significant sacrifices and embrace profound humility. Even though Jesus could have become an earthly king or messiah and gained relevance in the Jewish society of the time, Jesus chose to submit Himself to His Father's will. By surrendering His desires for relevance in society, Jesus became the King of Kings and is revered today as a shining example of obedience and humility. Following His example, we must prioritize obedience to God above all else and resist the temptation to conform to the expectations of the world around us. By doing so, we can find true purpose and live fulfilling lives.

Embrace Counter-Cultural Values

Your Christian nature requires you to acknowledge that your beliefs may not always align with societal norms or popular opinions. It is crucial to embrace counter-cultural values and stand firm in your convictions. This means being brave enough to go against the grain and hold onto your beliefs, even when they are unpopular or meet with resistance. By doing so, you can positively impact the world and live a life that is true to your faith.

Renew Your Mind

Protect your mind from negative influences and peer pressure. You can do this by focusing on authentic, noble, just, pure, lovely, and praiseworthy things, as stated in Philippians 4:8. Surround yourself with people who share your beliefs and can support and encourage you in your commitment to Christ. This will help you to renew your mind and stay on the right path. Remember to guard your thoughts and be mindful of what you allow into your mind.

Seek God's Approval

Due to our human nature, we are wired to seek approval and validation from others to feel accepted and valued. However, seeking God's approval should be our ultimate goal. His opinion should hold more weight than any other, and we should strive to live in a way that pleases Him. While the world may offer temporary approval, God's approval lasts forever. Therefore, we should seek His approval in every aspect of our lives. Jesus focused on the values of God's kingdom rather than conforming to the world's standards of relevance and power. He taught about humility, love, forgiveness, and service, demonstrating that true greatness lies in selfless devotion to God and others.

Serve with Humility

To serve humbly, we must cultivate a servant's heart and maintain a selfless attitude toward others. Striving for relevance can often cloud our judgment and prevent us from recognizing the needs of those around us. Instead, we should seek opportunities to serve others and improve their lives. One of the best ways to reflect Christ's love is through acts of compassion, kindness, and generosity, whether it's lending a listening ear to someone who needs to be heard, helping someone with their groceries or yard work, or volunteering at a sanctuary, church, or homeless shelter. There are countless ways to show love and kindness to those in need. By cultivating a servant's heart and reflecting Christ's love through our actions, we can positively impact the world and bring joy and hope to those who need it most.

Remember Your Identity in Christ

We all feel the pressure to conform to society's standards. However, our worth and significance do not come from how well we fit into the world's mold. Instead, as followers of Christ, we must ground our identity in Him. By doing so, we acknowledge that we are God's beloved children and that He is the source of our value. Jesus found His identity and significance in being God's Son rather than seeking validation from others. He did not depend on worldly recognition or fame but remained secure in His relationship with the Father. This allowed Jesus to resist the allure of seeking relevance through worldly means.

As disciples, our identity is in Christ. This means that we focus on our relationship with Him rather than on the opinions and expectations of others. We must find comfort in the knowledge that our relevance in the eyes of the world does not determine our worth. Instead, it comes from our status as God's children, which is unchanging and eternal. Let us hold fast to our identity in Christ and seek to live in a way that honors Him. Only through Jesus can we find our place in this world and experience the fullness of life that He intends for us.

Seek the Holy Spirit's Leading

To live a life that honors God, seeking the Holy Spirit's leading is essential. Depending on the Holy Spirit's guidance and empowerment can enable you to discern God's will and navigate the pressures of relevance. The Holy Spirit can transform your heart and renew your mind, giving you the courage and strength to live a life that is pleasing to God (Rom 12:2). Through the Holy Spirit, we can better understand what God wants from us and how we can make choices that align with His will. Therefore, seek the Holy Spirit's leading and allow Him to guide your path toward a life that honors God.

Overcoming the temptation to prioritize relevance requires a conscious and constant devotion to following Christ with all your heart. As you make obedience to God your top priority and seek His approval above everything else, you will discover genuine fulfillment and purpose in your journey of discipleship. Jesus remained unwavering in His faithfulness to His mission, even in the face of challenges and rejection. He understood His purpose was to save humanity through His sacrificial death and resurrection, and He never compromised that mission for earthly relevance. Through His steadfast commitment to God's will, Jesus demonstrated that true significance and relevance come from aligning your life with God's purpose. He resisted the temptation to seek worldly fame or relevance, choosing instead to fulfill His calling as the Messiah and Savior. By following Jesus's example, disciples can also overcome the temptation to prioritize relevance and instead focus on faithfully serving God and others according to His divine plan.

The Desire for Fame

The third leading temptation we face is the desire to be famous. As Christians, we are exposed to many temptations, but the pursuit of fame has become increasingly prevalent and destructive in recent years. Many Christian disciples are eager to gain fame and will do anything to achieve it. The advent of technology, especially social media platforms, has exacerbated this temptation by increasing the desire for instant gratification and applause. Moving away from the dominant self-made image often associated with fame-seeking is critical to counter this temptation. Christian leaders should take up the commission of "feeding my sheep," as Christ demanded from His disciples, recognizing that ministry is not only a communal experience but also a mutual experience. This means abstaining from working alone in ministry, projecting yourself over the team, or taking on the glory. This can only be achieved by working together with selfless service in the ministry.

Henri Nouwen's teachings emphasize refraining from the self-made image and moving toward a more community-oriented approach. This requires us to be accountable to the core members without holding back our wounded selves. It involves confession and forgiveness but also selfless service through the work of the Holy Spirit. Therefore, to follow the call to feed Christ's sheep without craving fame, we must cultivate an attitude of "more of Christ and the less of me." This discipline requires one to appreciate the role of confession and forgiveness, which allows us to join the flock in their experiences rather than hiding behind a veil of perfection. While it is unnecessary to lay all of our sins before our people, we must be accountable to the core members of the ministry without holding back.

There are several instances in the Bible where the desire for fame tempted people. One example is the story of the Tower of Babel in Genesis 11. The people of Babel were united in their will and passion to build a tower to extend to the heavens, as they wished to make a name for themselves. Their desire for fame and glory led to their downfall when God confused their language and scattered them across the world.

In the New Testament, the Pharisees were also tempted by the desire for fame and recognition. Jesus warned His disciples about their hypocrisy: "Everything they do is done for people to see: They make their phylacteries wide and the tassels on their garments long. They love the place of honor at banquets and the most important seats in the synagogues; they love to be greeted with respect in the marketplaces and called 'Rabbi' by others" (Mt 23:5–7). The Pharisees' desire for fame and recognition led them to prioritize their status over the needs of the people they were supposed to serve. Overall, the Bible warns against the temptation to seek fame and glory for ourselves. Instead, we are called to humble ourselves before God and prioritize obedience to His will above our desire for recognition and success.

How to Overcome the Fame-seeking Temptation

To overcome the temptation to seek fame, we must prioritize humility, a proper understanding of our identity as God's children, and a focus on serving God rather than seeking personal recognition. Here are some strategies to help overcome the desire to be famous.

Embrace Humility

Cultivate a humble attitude, recognizing that true greatness comes from serving others and following Christ's example. Release the desire for personal recognition and instead seek to honor God in everything that you do. Jesus embodied humility and constantly taught His disciples to prioritize humility over the desire for fame or prominence. He demonstrated this through His interactions with people, His choice of companions, and His willingness to serve others.

Reflect on the Nature of Fame

Fame, which is often fleeting and superficial, can be tempting, but it can also bring a plethora of challenges, pressures, and distractions. Constant media scrutiny and public expectations can create immense pressure, leading to anxiety and stress that can hinder spiritual growth. Moreover, pursuing fame can distract us from pursuing a Christ-centered life, leading us away from God's purpose for us. True fulfillment can only be found through a humble and virtuous life devoted to serving others and glorifying God. Instead of seeking fame and fortune, strive to align with Christ's teachings, focusing on love, compassion, humility, and selflessness. You can find true happiness and fulfillment by prioritizing God's will and purpose, regardless of your fame or worldly success.

Focus on Faithfulness

As believers, we must focus on faithfulness in our service to God and others, redirecting our energy from temporary recognition to the eternal reward of living a faithful life in service to Him. Jesus modeled faithfulness for us in His life and ministry, choosing to be a faithful servant and teacher who directed others to follow God. Through His teachings and example, Jesus emphasized the importance of faithfulness in discipleship, teaching us that faithfulness in serving God and others is of more value than temporary fame or recognition. In Matthew 25:23, Jesus affirms the faithfulness of His servant, praising him for being faithful with a few things and promising to put him in charge of many things.

This verse serves as a reminder that being faithful in small things leads to greater rewards in the future. Therefore, our primary goal as followers of Christ should be to serve God and others with faithfulness, knowing that our eternal reward far outweighs any temporary recognition we may receive by pursuing worldly fame. We must focus our energy and attention on following Christ and living out His teachings, just as He modeled a life of faithfulness and discipleship. Ultimately, our faithfulness in serving God and others will lead us to share in our master's happiness and receive our eternal reward.

Serve With a Pure Heart

As you embark on your journey of service and ministry, approach it with a pure heart. Your intentions should be focused on honoring God rather than seeking personal gain or fame. Your goal should be to bless and impact others without expecting recognition. Jesus was the ultimate example of selfless service and ministry. His teachings centered around God's kingdom's values—love, justice, mercy, and reconciliation. He encouraged His followers to prioritize these principles above all else rather than seeking fame or worldly success. Therefore, when you serve others, remember these values and strive to serve with a pure heart. This means your actions should be motivated by love, compassion, and a desire to impact others positively. By doing so, you will not only honor God but also inspire others to do the same.

Celebrate God's Work in Others

Christ's call is to love and celebrate each other's successes and achievements. Romans 12:10 instructs us to love each other with brotherly affection and to outdo one another in showing honor. This means we should seek opportunities to honor and celebrate God's work in our fellow believers' lives. Additionally, Philippians 2:3 reminds us not to act out of spite or arrogance but to consider others more significant than ourselves. Celebrating the work of others is an act of humility and generosity that reflects Christ's love.

When we uplift and encourage one another, we build a community that appreciates and celebrates people's outstanding contributions and gifts. Romans 12:15 says, "Rejoice with those who rejoice, weep with those who weep." This verse reminds us to share in the joy of others and to be present for them in their times of struggle. When we celebrate our fellow believers' successes, we create a culture of positivity and encouragement that strengthens our community and builds up our faith. Therefore, make it your aim to celebrate the outstanding work that God is doing in the lives of fellow believers and, in doing so, create a community of encouragement and positivity where everyone is valued and celebrated.

Cultivate Authentic Relationships

Building authentic relationships is becoming more challenging in today's fast-paced world, where online connections and social media platforms dominate communication. Authentic relationships are built on mutual trust, respect, and care. They require time, effort, and patience to develop and are different from transactional relationships, where people use each other for their benefit. To cultivate an authentic relationship, one must invest time in getting to know the other person on a deeper level and understanding their needs. This requires active listening and empathy to create a solid foundation of trust.

Authentic relationships are rooted in love and mutual growth in Christ, and they provide a sense of belonging, comfort, and support that is hard to find elsewhere. When we cultivate authentic relationships, we will foster meaningful connections that last a lifetime. These relationships provide a safe space where individuals can be vulnerable, share their thoughts and feelings, and seek guidance and support. Building genuine relationships is a crucial aspect of personal growth, and it helps us create a sense of purpose, joy, and fulfillment.

Surrender Your Desires to God

Lay your desires for fame at the feet of Jesus and surrender them to Him. Allow Him to shape your desires and redirect your ambitions toward His purposes. Pray for a heart satisfied with pursuing God's will rather than seeking worldly fame. Jesus consistently redirected honor and glory to God, emphasizing that all praise belongs to Him. He did not seek to promote Himself or accumulate fame but instead pointed people toward the Father.

Seek God's Direction

When making important decisions and navigating God's path, we must seek His guidance regularly. In doing so, we can trust that God has a unique plan and purpose for our lives, which may or may not involve worldly fame. Instead of seeking self-promotion, our focus should be on following His lead. The most inspiring example of this is the life of Jesus. He remained committed to fulfilling God's purpose for His life, even when it meant facing challenges and opposition. Despite the temptation to seek popularity or acclaim, Jesus prioritized obedience to the Father's will and sought to bring glory to God through His words and actions.

To stay connected to God's will and resist the world's distractions, Jesus regularly sought solitude and communion with God through prayer. This allowed Him to maintain a clear perspective on His mission, find strength in His relationship with the Father, and resist the allure of fame or recognition. We can follow Jesus's example by prioritizing our relationship with God and seeking His direction in every area of our lives. This means praying, studying the Bible, and listening for His voice. It also involves being open to His leading, even when it may mean going against our desires or expectations. Ultimately, seeking God's direction requires a deep trust in His plan for our lives. Proverbs 3:5–6 says, "Trust in the Lord with all your heart and lean not on your understanding; in all your ways submit to him, and he will make your paths straight." We can find true fulfillment and meaning in our lives by trusting God's guidance and staying committed to His purposes.

Root Your Identity in God

Jesus found His identity and self-worth in His relationship with God the Father. He knew He was God's Son, enabling Him to remain grounded and focused on His mission without needing worldly validation or recognition. Jesus consistently redirected attention and glory to God throughout His ministry rather than seeking personal recognition or fame.

This is evident in passages such as John 8:54–58, where Jesus affirms that His glory means nothing if He glorifies Himself. Instead, He emphasizes that God the Father is the one who glorifies Him. This demonstrates Jesus's deep reliance on God's validation and the importance of an identity rooted in our relationship with God. Moreover, in Matthew 3:17, we see God the Father affirming Jesus's identity and mission, declaring, "This is my Son, whom I love; with him, I am well pleased." This affirmation gave Jesus the confidence to carry out His mission, knowing He was loved and valued by God. We can learn from Jesus's example and strive to find our identity in our relationship with God rather than seeking validation from the world. When we prioritize our connection with God, we will remain grounded and focused on our mission to honor God, serve others, and reflect Christ's love in the world.

By embracing humility, seeking God's direction, and focusing on faithful service, you can overcome the temptation to seek fame and instead find fulfillment and purpose in following Christ. By embodying humility, prioritizing God's will, redirecting honor to God, and focusing on God's kingdom, Jesus overcame the temptation to seek fame. He also demonstrated that true significance comes from living aligned with God's purposes rather than pursuing worldly acclaim. We can learn from Jesus's example and seek to follow Him faithfully, finding our fulfillment and purpose in serving God and others.

The Desire for Power

The fourth leading temptation that Christian leaders face is the desire for power. Power is not evil, but it can become a dangerous temptation if we obsess over it. According to Nouwen, the temptation for power is one of the most powerful challenges for Christian leaders to overcome because it offers an easy substitute for the arduous task of love. Christian leaders may find it easier to control people than to love them. Such a leadership style may cause a leader to play God, seeking to discern where Christ wants them to go, even if that direction doesn't match Christ's will for their life.

To overcome this temptation, Christian leaders must employ a discipline that involves a profound, scripturally informed, and heavenly-minded reflection. Such discipline helps Christian leaders avoid becoming mere psychologists, motivational speakers, or social workers. It spurs them to reflect on joyful and painful realities with the mind of Christ. It also raises their consciousness about God's gentle guidance and authority. By being scripturally informed and heavenly-minded, Christian disciples can navigate the world's challenges, such as accidentalism, fatalism, incidentals, and defeatism, on their Christian journeys. Accidentalism refers to the idea that life's events are random and have no meaning or purpose. Fatalism, on the other hand, is the belief that everything is predetermined and there is nothing one can do to change it. Incidentals happen by chance, while defeatism is the belief that one is powerless against life's challenges.

Therefore, Christ's disciples must be well-informed, disciplined, and heavenly-minded to avoid pursuing power. This will enable them to lead with love, humility, and wisdom as they navigate life's challenges. This focus on love, humility, and wisdom sets Christian leaders apart and enables them to serve with humility, grace, and compassion.

In Matthew 4:8-9, we read about Christ's temptation by the devil to gain power over all the world's kingdoms. The devil takes Christ to a high mountain and shows Him all the kingdoms of the world in their splendor. This was a significant temptation for Jesus, as it presented an opportunity to gain power and influence on a global scale without going through the suffering and sacrifice of the cross.

This was not the first time Jesus faced temptation. The devil had already tempted Him to turn stones into bread and to test God's protection by jumping off the pinnacle of the temple. In both instances, Jesus responded with Scripture, saying, "Man shall not live by bread alone, but by every word that proceeds out of the mouth of God," and "You shall not tempt the Lord your God." However, the devil wasn't done yet. With the third temptation, he sought to appeal to Christ's desire for power and love for the world. Satan offered Christ every kingdom of the world and their magnificence if Christ would bow down and worship Him. This was a tempting offer, as it would have given Christ the power to rule over all the nations of the world with all the wealth and glory that came with it.

Jesus saw through the devil's deception and responded with the words, "Get behind me, Satan! For it is written, 'You shall worship the Lord your God, and him only shall you serve'" (Mt 4:10). This response shows that Jesus was not willing to compromise His allegiance to God for the sake of gaining worldly power and influence. He recognized that true power and influence come from serving and obeying God, not from bowing down to the devil. Satan's offer of power over all the world's kingdoms was a significant test of Christ's faith and commitment to God. However, Jesus remained faithful, choosing to follow God's will and serve Him alone. This demonstrates that true power and influence come from serving God and obeying His commands rather than seeking worldly power and wealth. It also reminds us that our approach to our walk with Jesus and our reflection of the gospel needs to change significantly. We must shift our attitude and way of life to embrace Christ's teachings and life.

One of the key areas that requires a shift in focus is our desire for relevance. Instead of striving to be relevant, we need to prioritize prayer. Doing so can strengthen our relationship with God and help us better understand His will for us. We also need to move away from our preoccupation with fame and status and instead focus on participating in communal ministry. This means prioritizing the needs of our community and working together to impact the world around us positively.

Furthermore, we must stop seeking power and instead strive to understand and discern God's will for ourselves and those we lead. This requires a deeper understanding of God's Word and a commitment to living in accordance with His teachings. When we abstain from these temptations, we will better reflect the gospel and follow in Jesus Christ's footsteps.

How to Overcome the Power-Seeking Temptation

To overcome the temptation to seek power, we must embrace the teachings and examples of Jesus, who demonstrated a servant-hearted approach to leadership. Here are some more steps to help overcome the temptation to seek power.

Embrace Humility

True greatness in God's kingdom comes through humility. Follow the example of Jesus, who humbled Himself and served others selflessly. Cultivate a humble attitude, acknowledging that all authority and power ultimately belong to God.

Study the Teachings of Jesus

Immerse yourself in the teachings of Jesus found in the Bible. Explore His teachings on servant leadership, love, and selflessness. Reflect on His interactions with others and His emphasis on sacrificial service. Jesus consistently redirected attention and honor to God rather than seeking it for Himself. He displayed humility and taught His disciples not to seek prominence or recognition.

Seek God's Will

Prioritize aligning your desires with God's will rather than pursuing power or ambition. Spend time in prayer, seeking God's guidance, and surrendering your ambitions and plans to Him. Ask for His strength to resist the temptation to seek power. In the gospels, Jesus emphasizes the values of God's kingdom, which contrast with the world's understanding of power. He teaches about love, humility, compassion, and self-sacrifice. His teachings challenge the world's pursuit of power and demonstrate a completely different way of living and leading.

Examine Your Motives

As you contemplate pursuing power and influence, delve deeper into your motives and intentions. Take the time to reflect on your desires and ask yourself if they align with Jesus' teachings and values. Examine whether your pursuit of power is driven by a sincere desire to serve and bring glory to God or if it is motivated by selfish ambition and the thirst for personal gain. Consider your actions' impact on others and whether they align with the principles of love, compassion, and humility that Jesus embodied.

In addition, could you evaluate the potential consequences of your pursuit of power? Will it lead to the empowerment of others and the advancement of God's kingdom, or will it lead to the exploitation of others and self-glorification? By taking a comprehensive and reflective approach, you can ensure that your pursuit of power is rooted in righteousness and guided by a genuine desire to serve others and bring glory to God. This will help you to avoid the pitfalls of pride and ego and instead focus on using your power and influence for the greater good.

Serve Others

Shift your focus from seeking power to serving others. Look for opportunities to serve and bless those around you—practice acts of kindness, compassion, and generosity. Seek to meet others' needs rather than seeking personal gain or influence. Jesus redefined the concept of power by exemplifying servant leadership. He taught that true greatness comes from serving others rather than lording power over them. He washed His disciples' feet to demonstrate this principle, a symbol of humility and servanthood.

Surrender Control to God

Let go of the need to control outcomes. Instead, trust God's sovereignty. Recognize that true power comes from relying on the Holy Spirit and allowing God to work through you. Surrender your desire for personal power and submit to God's guidance and direction. Jesus surrendered Himself to the Father's will. He recognized that true power comes from being aligned with God's purposes rather than seeking power for its own sake. He regularly sought God's guidance and direction in His ministry. Jesus relied on the Holy Spirit's power to carry out His mission rather than relying on earthly power or influence. This allowed Him to resist the temptation to seek power for self-glorification.

Surround Yourself with Like-Minded Believers

To help you follow in Jesus's footsteps and live a life of servant leadership, surround yourself with believers who share your values and beliefs. Seek out a community of disciples passionate about serving others and committed to living out the gospel message.

Connect with these individuals and build genuine relationships based on mutual trust and support. Encourage one another to resist the temptation to seek power and instead focus on serving others with humility and compassion. Share your struggles and challenges, and hold each other accountable to live a life of service.

Through this deep and meaningful connection with fellow believers, you can grow your faith and become a true ambassador of Christ's love and grace. Together, you can make a difference in the world by shining a light of hope and compassion and serving as an example of what it means to be a servant leader. Implementing this idea includes joining a small group or Bible study at your church where members are committed to serving others and following the example of Jesus's servant leadership. You can also seek opportunities to volunteer with local organizations that align with your values and beliefs and invite other like-minded believers to join you. Additionally, you can connect with fellow Christians through online communities or social media groups to share your thoughts, experiences, and challenges with others who share your passion for servant leadership and humble service.

Reflect Regularly on Christ's Examples

Make a habit of regularly contemplating the examples set by Jesus Christ. His life was marked by sacrifice, and He called upon His followers to walk the path of discipleship. To truly internalize His teachings, reflecting on His example and allowing it to shape your thoughts and actions is critical to your discipleship. By meditating on His humility, love, and selflessness, you can gain a deeper understanding of His message and apply it to your life. So, take the time to reflect regularly on Christ's examples and strive to live a life of love and service.

Seek Inner Transformation

Allow the Holy Spirit to transform your heart and character. Invite the Holy Spirit to work in you, shaping you into someone who reflects Christ's character. Pray for God's power to be evident in your life through the fruit of the spirit—love, patience, kindness, joy, peace, goodness, faithfulness, gentleness, and self-control (Gal 5:22).

Nonviolent Resistance

Jesus was known for His teachings of nonviolence and peaceful resistance. He taught that love, forgiveness, and reconciliation are the most potent tools to assert His authority instead of force or violence. His life and teachings are a testament to the power of nonviolent resistance, as He willingly endured immense suffering and laid down His life for the redemption of humanity. His message of love and peace resonates with millions of people worldwide.

An example of Jesus's nonviolent resistance to power is His response to His arrest in the Garden of Gethsemane. One of His disciples, Simon Peter, pulled his sword and struck the high priest's servant, slicing off his ear. In response, Jesus told him to "put his sword away and reminded him that those who live by the sword will also die by it" (Mt 26:52). The message is clear: violence only begets more violence, and it is better to seek peace and understanding than resort to aggression. Jesus's response demonstrates His commitment to nonviolence, even in the face of arrest and persecution, and shows that love and forgiveness can be more potent than violence.

Reject Worldly Temptations

Jesus resisted the allure of worldly power offered by Satan during His temptation in the wilderness. He chose not to pursue power through shortcuts or compromises. Instead, He remained steadfast in His commitment to follow God's ways. By embracing humility, serving others, and seeking God's will, you can overcome the temptation to seek power and instead embody the servant-hearted leadership modeled by Jesus. Remember that true power comes from surrendering to God and allowing Him to work through you for His purposes.

Jesus exemplified a unique understanding of power rooted in humility, love, and selflessness through His life, teachings, and sacrifice on the cross. He overcame the temptation to pursue power for personal gain, instead embodying a power that seeks the well-being and transformation of others. By following Jesus's example, you can also overcome the temptation to seek power and embrace a Christlike approach to leadership that prioritizes service, love, and the advancement of God's kingdom. Always remember that the power to resist these temptations lies within us.

Note

[1] Henri J. M. Nouwen, *In the Name of Jesus: Reflections on Christian Leadership* (Crossroad Faith & Formation, 1992).

For Reflection

1. What are some of the biggest temptations you face as a disciple, and how do they affect your spiritual growth?

2. In a society that values material wealth, power, and fame, avoiding the desire for these things can be challenging. However, succumbing to these pursuits can negatively affect your personal and professional life. How would you describe your struggle with these desires, and what steps can you take to overcome them?

3. How would you describe your struggle with materialism and the desire for wealth and possessions? Are there specific areas or situations where this struggle is more pronounced?

4. As you reflect on this chapter, consider the insights you have gained about overcoming temptation. What strategies and practices did you discover that can help you in your Christian life?

5. How can you integrate these teachings into your daily life and build on them to become more spiritually grounded and resilient?

Food For Thought

Despite the diverse faith teachings, doctrines, and beliefs, such as those of atheists, secularists, and other religions, Christians still get to believe and do what the Bible reveals about God's will, morality, and proper behavior.

Four

THE ROLE OF THE WORD IN DISCIPLESHIP

> *All scripture is inspired by God and useful for teaching, reproof, correction, and training in righteousness so that everyone who belongs to God may be proficient—moreover, equipped for every good work.*[1]
>
> **2 Timothy 3:16**

The Bible is critical for identifying themes, truths, and messages that are essential for Christian living. It also provides guidelines on why Christians should recognize certain scriptures in various aspects of their lives. In addition, the Bible is a whole of epic stories that establish the glory of the Messiah, His promises, and the truth about humankind. The Bible also teaches us about various themes and topics, such as sin, redemption, angels, cherubim, and seraphim, which helps Christians to relate to such things in contemporary life.[2] Hence, we must discuss the role of the Bible in Christianity and practice. Before we move forward, however, some insights into the Bible's authenticity and canonicity will be beneficial.

The Bible consists of sacred texts a particular religious community unanimously considers authentic and authoritative. Christians believe the canonical books or manuscripts are inspired by God and express the definitive narrative of how God relates to His people. Arnold and Beyer satisfy our quest for certainty on the authoritative nature of the Bible when they accentuate "the importance of distinguishing between the Old Testament books of the Bible that came directly from God and those that emanated from the human author's understanding. Arnold and Beyer focused on three determinants to consider when testing for canonicity. The three factors are 'the author, audience, and teaching.'"[3]

The first determinant is whether the authors wrote the text under the Holy Spirit's leadership. The second determinant is whether they wrote these books for people of all generations. If God inspired the writing, it must be relevant and applicable to people of all ages. The third factor addresses the teachings themselves. They must not contradict one another; instead, each teaching should provide more revelation, interacting with other teachings. Knowledge of the Bible's canonicity goes beyond mere solidification of our foundational and biblical knowledge. It also enhances our spiritual development by helping us understand that God is the ultimate Author of the Bible, the One who inspired the writers and allowed them to express their personalities as they wrote.

The New Testament contains an important message from the Apostle Paul emphasizing the divine inspiration of all scripture. Paul believed that the Bible is not just a collection of words but rather a means of communication directly from God. He taught that all scripture is useful for teaching, reproof, correction, and training in righteousness (2 Tim 3:16–17). This means the Bible can guide us in living a righteous and just life and correct us when we go astray. Paul believed that the purpose of scripture is to equip God's people with the knowledge and skills needed to do good works. He taught that by reading and studying the scriptures, we can become proficient and well-prepared to perform any good work God calls us to do. The clarity and profound truth about the canonicity of the Old Testament, along with Paul's emphasis on the authoritative nature of all scripture, is a source of courage and confidence for those who seek to learn, teach, and preach God's Word. Through the scriptures, we can better understand God's will and purpose for our lives and find the strength and guidance to do His work in the world.

The Bible is a robust and comprehensive guidebook for Christians, providing specific answers to questions related to Christian theology. It encompasses a wealth of knowledge and wisdom that can deepen our understanding of God's plan for humanity and prepare us for the Messiah's return. By studying the Bible, we can gain insights into why certain books were written in a particular way and how the historical and cultural context of the specific revelation of God's people impacted its message. This deeper understanding allows us to grasp the significance of the Bible's teachings and apply them to our lives.

Through the Bible's teachings, Christians can discover the Messiah's true identity and understand why He is considered the Son of God. The Bible clearly shows Jesus's relationship with God and how Christ's life, death, and resurrection fulfilled Old Testament prophecies. Furthermore, the covenant relationship by which God has united Himself to His people through Jesus Christ is explained in great detail in the Bible, particularly in Acts 28:23. By understanding the nature of this covenant, Christians can gain a deeper appreciation for God's love and grace and how it has been extended to us through Jesus Christ. This strong foundation of knowledge and understanding provides us with the necessary tools to correct any teachings that may be false or misleading and to stay true to our faith. The Bible is an indispensable resource for Christians seeking to deepen their relationship with God and live a fulfilling, purpose-driven life.

In addition, Christians can find confidence and truth in the Holy Scriptures regarding marriage and family matters. The Bible offers comprehensive guidance on building strong and healthy marriage and family relationships. It provides a framework for how spouses should treat each other, their roles in the marriage relationship, and the importance of love, respect, and forgiveness. The Bible emphasizes that marriage is a sacred covenant between a man and a woman, designed to reflect the love and commitment between Christ and the Church. As such, the Bible provides a holistic approach to marriage, offering guidance on everything from communication and conflict resolution to intimacy and parenting.

Ephesians 5:21–33 teaches us about submitting to one another out of reverence for Christ. Specifically, wives are called to submit to their husbands, as they would to the Lord, for the husband is the head of his wife, just as Christ is the head of the Church. As the Church submits to Christ, wives should submit to their husbands in everything. Meanwhile, husbands are commanded to love their wives just as Christ loves the Church, even to the extent of laying down their lives for their spouses. This passage emphasizes the importance of mutual respect and love between husbands and wives, as modeled by the relationship between Christ and the Church. This passage also teaches husbands to prioritize their wives' needs, to be selfless and sacrificial in their love, and to cherish and honor their wives as precious gifts from God. Similarly, Colossians 3:18–19 says wives are instructed to submit to their husbands and encourages husbands to love their wives and not be harsh with them. These passages promote mutual respect, understanding, and communication between spouses, emphasizing the importance of teamwork in building a healthy and happy marriage.

Moreover, the Bible offers practical advice on raising children and building strong family bonds. Proverbs 22:6 instructs parents to train their children in how they should go so that when their children grow up, they will not depart from it. This passage emphasizes the importance of instilling values, principles, morals, and beliefs in children from a young age, teaching them to respect and honor their parents, to love God and others, and to live a life that reflects Christ's teachings. Additionally, the Bible guides discipline, instruction, and correction, emphasizing the importance of consistency, fairness, and love in shaping a child's character and behavior. The Bible provides a comprehensive and timeless guide for building strong and healthy family relationships. Its teachings emphasize the importance of love, respect, forgiveness, communication, teamwork, and partnership in building a happy and fulfilling home. By following the Bible's principles and teachings, couples can strengthen their relationships, deepen their faith, and create a solid and lasting bond that honors God and reflects the beauty and sanctity of marriage.

The Bible also contains several teachings regarding work and leisure, emphasizing the importance of both. The Bible encourages hard work and the satisfaction of a job well done. Ecclesiastes 3:13 states that finding satisfaction in our toil is a gift from God, and Proverbs 14:23 emphasizes the importance of hard work to achieve profit. However, the Bible also recognizes the need for rest, self-care, and recreation. Ecclesiastes 8:15 encourages us to enjoy life and find joy in our work, acknowledging that taking time to relax and recharge is essential. The concept of the Sabbath is central to Jewish and Christian traditions, which involves dedicating one day a week to rest and worship.

Furthermore, the Bible also emphasizes the right attitude toward work. Colossians 3:23–24 states that we should work as if we are working for the Lord, not for humans, and that we will be rewarded for doing so. This encourages us to work with integrity and honesty, recognizing that our work reflects our faith. It also helps us remember that our work is ultimately for God's glory. The Bible plays a crucial role in the spiritual and moral well-being of the Church. Ephesians 2:20 emphasizes the vital role of the apostles and prophets in laying the foundation of the house of God. The cornerstone of this foundation is none other than Christ Jesus Himself. The Bible guides prophets and leaders in the Church, emphasizing the importance of the Church as a place that welcomes people and is life-giving. It serves as a source of inspiration and direction to believers, guiding them toward a deeper understanding of the Church's purpose and mission.

The Bible offers a comprehensive perspective on various theological topics, including the nature of God, the meaning of life, and the relationship between humanity and divinity. It provides a clear and precise understanding of God's will and teachings, which is essential in shaping the Christian worldview. Despite the existence of diverse faiths and beliefs in our modern societies, Christians still hold onto the Bible's teachings on morality and proper behavior in society. The Bible provides a timeless and universal standard of ethics and values that speaks to the heart of every human being, regardless of their cultural or religious background.

The Bible is not just a book of ancient wisdom or a historical artifact. It is a living and dynamic source of guidance and inspiration that continues to shape and transform the lives of millions of believers worldwide. It is an essential part of the Christian faith and a priceless treasure that should be cherished and protected for future generations.

Additionally, the Bible instructs Christians to respect the governing authorities by selecting a suitable candidate and prioritizing voting. Specifically, in Romans 13, Christians are taught to submit to the governing authorities because God established them. This means that Christians should obey the laws of the land while participating in the democratic process by voting for leaders who align with their values.

The Bible is a comprehensive guide for Christians, providing wisdom and guidance on everything from personal relationships to societal issues. God's message is the foundation of truth. And Christians are expected to apply it to every aspect of their lives. For instance, Christians are called to love their neighbors as themselves and to care for the poor and marginalized in their communities.

Christians must learn and apply God's teachings in their personal lives and seek to impact the world around them positively. By prioritizing voting and engaging in acts of service, Christians can fulfill their responsibility to God and their fellow human beings. As we encounter complex issues such as sex, homosexuality, drugs, abortion, cloning, and emerging scientific concerns, it's crucial to approach them with a discerning mind and a heart rooted in faith. Understanding and accepting God's perspective can build a solid foundation for navigating these challenges. Incorporating unwavering faith and trust in our decision-making process allows us to make choices and take actions that align with our beliefs and values.

For disciples, applying biblical principles is essential when making decisions about sex, homosexuality, drugs, abortion, gender, cloning, and emerging scientific concerns like AI. By relying on God's Word, we can gain insight into what is right and wrong and make choices that promote righteousness and justice. Aligning ourselves with God's will enables us to approach these issues with clarity, confidence, and a sense of purpose. By doing so, we can make informed decisions that align with our beliefs and values, promote righteousness and justice, and ultimately honor God. The question that comes to mind is, "If the Bible is so good, why are some people against its teachings?"

There are various reasons why some people are against the Bible. Some reject it because they disagree with its teachings, while others have had negative experiences with individuals or communities who claim to follow the Bible. Some may view the Bible as an outdated or irrelevant text that has no place in modern society. Others reject it due to personal beliefs or experiences that conflict with its teachings. For followers of Christ, it is paramount to approach these situations with compassion and understanding, seeking to engage in respectful dialogue and to address concerns and questions with honesty and humility. Doing so can build bridges of understanding and promote greater harmony and unity within our communities.

Notes

[1] 2 Tim 3:16 (New Revised Standard Version).

[2] Alister McGrath, *Christian Theology: An Introduction* (Atlanta: Wiley-Blackwell, 2010).

[3] Bill T. Arnold and Bryan E. Beyer, *Encountering the Old Testament: a Christian Survey* (Grand Rapids, MI: Baker Academic, 2015), 3.

For Reflection

1. How does the Word of God influence your decisions and actions as you go about your day-to-day activities? In what ways has it brought about a transformation in your perspectives, attitudes, and behaviors?

2. When you come across Bible passages that seem to contradict or challenge your personal beliefs or worldview, what steps do you take to understand and interpret them?

3. How do you perceive the Word of God in relation to other sources of knowledge and/or wisdom? Do you consider it the ultimate authority or just one of many sources you consult for guidance and understanding?

4. Over the years, how has your comprehension and interpretation of the Word of God evolved and expanded? Can you identify the factors that have significantly impacted this growth?

Food for Thought

A just ruler leads to a prosperous society, while an unjust ruler leads to suffering. As responsible citizens, we must support leaders who prioritize fairness, equality, and biblical principles. Let us choose wise and just leaders for a better future.

Five

THE ROLE OF POLITICS IN A CHRISTIAN'S LIFE

<blockquote>
When righteous individuals hold positions of power, the general population experiences joy and happiness.

Proverb 29:2
</blockquote>

Are Christians Morally Obligated to Consider Politics?

Societies thrive under the rule of just and fair leaders who value equality and promote the well-being of their people. Such leaders ensure that their citizens experience safety, security, and success. On the other hand, unjust rulers bring misery and suffering to their people. As responsible citizens, we must support leaders who prioritize our well-being and that of the community. Let us choose wisely and elect just leaders for a better future. When individuals in positions of power are honest, empathetic, and act with integrity, it creates a ripple effect that benefits society, fostering an environment of trust, transparency, and accountability.

Citizens feel secure and stable, knowing their leaders are working toward the greater good. This, in turn, leads to a more engaged and participative citizenry who are willing to contribute their time and resources toward improving society. The result is a virtuous cycle of progress and development, where everyone works together to achieve common goals and create a brighter future. Good government enables churches to teach and preach the truth. Government organizations play a vital role in advancing the gospel and the welfare of others. Proper regulations help to promote education, encourage the establishment of just laws, and grant religious liberty. Christian witness in public administration also contributes to transcending values about ethical and moral issues.

Politics has a significant impact on the government, society, and culture. This influence is inescapable, so it is necessary to consider the role of politics in our lives. The Bible is an authoritative guiding force that has a lasting effect on our culture. This effect obligates Christians to consider politics as a crucial aspect of life. As governing establishments continue to shape our world, it is becoming increasingly vital for Christians to project a Christian worldview in the political sphere. By participating in the political process, we can contribute toward establishing a just and fair society that reflects the values of our faith.

The relationship between politics and Christianity is complicated and has long been discussed among scholars and theologians. Although Christianity does not offer a direct political program, the Bible's narratives are replete with political themes that shed light on the relationship between faith and government. Renowned scholar Francis J. Beckwith has argued that the Bible provides fundamental principles Christians can use to understand their role in politics and political institutions.[1] These principles are based on theological and philosophical concepts that help construct a Christian vision of government administration. For instance, the Bible emphasizes justice, which is integral to any political system, and the importance of freedom, which enables individuals to exercise their God-given rights. The Bible also highlights the role of the family in society, which is central to a healthy social order. Moreover, the Bible's fundamental theological and philosophical ideas about the nature of God and reality are crucial in shaping a government administration rooted in a Christian worldview. These ideas include the significance of human beings, created in the image of God, to flourish and serve God's eternal providence. The Bible offers rich principles that help Christians understand the relationship between politics and their faith.

Christian involvement in politics has been a topic of controversy, with some people arguing that anything apart from clear teaching and preaching of the Bible is a diversion from the church's mission. However, this perspective offers a limited understanding of God's kingdom and fails to consider the examples in the Holy Scriptures. The Bible discusses civil government and provides examples of faithful engagement, such as Daniel, Joseph, and Esther. As "good and faithful Christians" (1 Peter 2:11), we may be tempted to think that secular political systems are inappropriate tools for spreading the gospel. However, this perspective is shortsighted. Consider a pastor or minister in an underground church or a missionary trying to spread the gospel across borders. Passports, religious liberties, and travel visas are not just luxuries but necessities in these situations. Reaching people in certain parts of the world may be impossible without them.

A Christian worldview should recognize that political engagement is essential for addressing all areas of life, including social justice issues, human rights, and freedom. We have a responsibility to advocate for justice and promote the common good. This is why many Christians are involved in public affairs, seeking positive societal change. Contrary to popular arguments, I contend that Christian political engagement is not a distraction from the church's mission. Instead, it is essential to fulfilling the Great Commission, which calls us to make disciples of all nations. Christians must comprehensively understand reality and engage in political processes to promote justice, freedom, and well-being.

Understanding Christians' Moral Obligation Toward Politics

Francis J. Beckwith's book *Politics for Christians*[2] delves into why Christians have a moral obligation to engage in politics. The book covers four crucial areas, which include (1) Caesar's coin and the image of God; (2) doing justice; (3) knowing your government, its laws, and the scope of your citizenship; and (4) voting for and supporting Christian candidates. Beckwith offers biblical and theological perspectives on these topics to help Christians understand their role in politics.

The "coin" represents the earthly government, a human institution established to maintain order and protect citizens. The "image of God" means that every human being is created in the image of God and, therefore, has inherent worth and dignity. Beckwith argues that Christians, as God's image-bearers, should participate in politics because it affects the lives of their fellow citizens, who are also image-bearers.[3]

Doing justice involves not only individual acts of kindness and charity but also a concern for the public culture and tradition and how they impact the citizens' virtue. "Christians are called to be concerned about how our public culture is being shaped and formed."[4] This means Christians should be involved in the political process to influence the laws and policies affecting their lives. We should deeply understand what our citizenship entails, encompassing our rights, duties, and responsibilities. This requires us to remain informed about the laws that govern our country as well as the social and political issues that affect us.

Participation in the political process is vital for representing our values and worldview in the government. This involvement can involve participating in the electoral process, voting during elections, reaching out to our elected representatives, and peacefully demonstrating to make our voices heard. Christians must endorse candidates who align with their beliefs and promote policies that protect the sanctity of life, preserve the traditional family, and safeguard religious freedom. While support is essential, consider endorsing candidates who share our values and strive to promote justice, human dignity, and the common good. This will enable us to contribute toward building a fair and impartial society.

A government that is genuinely concerned about its citizens' welfare is essential for the greater good of society. Similarly, citizens believe a just government is the most suitable one to maintain their well-being, guarantee peace, and drive economic growth. This argument is supported by Proverbs 29:2, which states, "When the righteous are in authority, the people rejoice." Despite their separate jurisdictions, the church and the government have a shared obligation to promote human welfare.

Christians have a moral responsibility to promote justice and ensure that the culture and traditions we share do not compromise our virtue. Christians must be mindful of how the culture is shaped, given that politics directly impacts evangelism, charity, and missionary work. To this end, Christians should utilize their legitimate authority and take political action to support laws and policies that promote peace and stability, which are fundamental prerequisites for human flourishing. By doing so, Christians can uphold their moral obligation to promote justice and contribute to the betterment of society.

In his thought-provoking article, "Tolerance Without Compromise," Richard J. Mouw delves into the complex relationship between Christianity and politics. He provides invaluable guidance for Christians struggling to reconcile their faith with political beliefs. Drawing on his experiences as a graduate student in the 1960s, Mouw emphasizes the importance of Christian involvement in politics despite the challenges and conflicts that may arise. He contends that Christians are morally obligated to participate in politics and help shape public discourse through civil justice. He references John Calvin's belief that engagement in public life allows us to develop virtues such as civility, humility, and involvement. Mouw argues that this obligation is compatible with a Christian worldview and that the Christian faith provides the best resources for cultivating these virtues.

Mouw's article is a call to action for Christians to engage in public conversations and promote positive values in the political sphere. He encourages Christians to be responsible citizens and use their faith to guide their political beliefs and actions. Overall, Mouw's piece is a timely reminder of the importance of Christian involvement in politics and provides valuable insights for anyone grappling with the relationship between faith and politics.

Alvin Schmidt's book How Christianity Changed the World[5] is another insightful documentation of the Christian influence in government. The book provides a comprehensive understanding of the moral obligations of Christians toward politics and public office. Schmidt contends that Christ's followers brought revolutionary changes that impacted various aspects of society, including social, political, economic, and cultural spheres. He provides numerous examples of the positive influence of Christianity, such as the outlawing of infanticide and child abandonment, ending the tradition of human sacrifice among European cultures, banning polygamy and pedophilia, and forbidding the burning of widows in India.

Dr. Paul L. Maier, a professor of ancient history, acknowledges that the Christian faith has been the most influential agent in reconstructing society for over two thousand years since Jesus's life on Earth.[6] He also notes how Christianity has played a consequential function in shaping the world's history, as it continues to do so today. Schmidt also notes that the impact of Christ's followers on society has been revolutionary, transforming social, political, economic, and cultural norms.[7]

Over time, some Christians began to recognize slavery as a stark violation of Christian values and principles. Among these stalwart abolitionists was William Wilberforce, an influential member of England's House of Commons. Wilberforce's dedication led to the abolition of the slave trade in England. The United States also saw the emergence of a robust abolitionist undertaking, with two-thirds of abolitionists in the mid-1830s being Christian clergy members. This group of determined abolitionists played a substantial role in the struggle against slavery. Martin Luther King Jr., a renowned and heroic Christian pastor, emerged as a critical figure in the civil rights movement, leading the crusade against racial discrimination and injustice.

Carl F. H. Henry, an American evangelical theologian, believed Christians should engage with civil authorities to promote justice and the common good, providing critical insights, personal examples, and vocational leadership.[8] Schmidt's observations show that Christianity has driven many positive social changes throughout history. These inspiring revolutionary changes will continue as Christians participate in all levels of society.

Christianity and Politics: Are They Scripturally Compatible?

This question requires a detailed examination. In the Old Testament, David, Josiah, Daniel, Esther, and Joseph served in public government to promote their people's well-being and make God known in all aspects of their lives. These leaders used their influence to bring about positive change in their communities.

Although not directly involved in the government, Christ's ministry was a model of holistic care and compassion, as He is the King of all Kings. He attended to the emotional, physical, and spiritual needs of those around Him—feeding the hungry, healing the sick, and performing miracles to demonstrate His love. His ministry was grounded in His profound comprehension of human suffering and His commitment to help those in need regardless of their social status or background. His example of service and selflessness has inspired generations of Christians to follow in His footsteps and work toward a more just and compassionate world.

Following Christ's example, the Apostle Paul also emphasized the importance of doing good to everyone. In his letter to the Galatians, he underscores the moral responsibility of extending positivity and compassion to others. This responsibility includes every individual we encounter daily, regardless of background, beliefs, or values. It is imperative that we make a special effort to show compassion and generosity toward those who share our faith. Doing so can strengthen our sense of community, foster mutual respect and understanding, and create a more harmonious and peaceful society (Gal 6:10).

In his letter to the Ephesians, Paul stresses that the Christian faith teaches us that we are created in Christ Jesus for a specific purpose. This purpose is not limited to our salvation but extends to the good works God has prepared us to engage in. These good works encompass a wide range of activities that align with God's will and aim to bring glory to Him. They include ministering to the needy, giving to charity, spreading the gospel, and simply showing kindness and love to those around us. These good works are not a way to earn salvation but an expression of our faith as we manifest the fruit of the Spirit. As believers, we have been saved by grace through faith, and our good works are simply the evidence of that faith. They are a way of showing the world that we belong to Christ and that His love has transformed our lives (Eph 2:10). I encourage you to embrace this theology, which recognizes that every area of life, including politics, can be a way to do good works and put our faith into action.

The rulings made by our government have a significant impact on people's lives and how we relate to one another. Therefore, engaging in the political process is one way to participate in doing good works. While not everyone is qualified or able to run for public office, we can all participate by voting or showing our support for a candidate. The character of a society's leaders determines the happiness and well-being of society. When virtuous individuals hold positions of power, people experience joy and contentment. However, when corrupt and malevolent figures take control, people suffer and lament (Prov 29:2). Ultimately, as followers of Christ, we must strive to positively impact every area of life, including politics, by doing good works that honor God and benefit our communities.

Notes

[1] F. J. Beckwith, *Politics for Christians: Statecraft as Soulcraft* (Downers Grove, IL: IVP Academic, 2010).

[2] Ibid.

[3] Ibid.

[4] Ibid.

[5] A. J. Schmidt, *How Christianity Changed the World* (Grand Rapids, MI: Zondervan, 2004).

[6] Dr. Paul L. Maier is a professor of ancient history. He taught at Western Michigan University for fifty-one years and was also the campus chaplain for thirty-nine of those years.

[7] A. J. Schmidt, (2004).

[8] Carl F. H. Henry is an American evangelical theologian.

For Reflection

1. How do your Christian beliefs impact your political views and decisions? How do you reconcile your personal values and biblical principles with your political support?

2. How can you ensure that your political involvement aligns with biblical principles such as righteousness, justice, compassion, and humility?

3. In today's often polarized political climate, finding ways to engage in fruitful discussions with those who hold different views is paramount. How can we approach political issues and events in a way that shows respect and love for others, even when we disagree?

4. As you contemplate your involvement in politics, consider the bigger picture and how your actions fit into God's grand design for the world. What is the purpose of your political engagement, and how is it contributing to a more harmonious and just society that aligns with God's values?

Notes

Section Two

THE CHARACTERISTICS OF A
TRUE DISCIPLE

Food For Thought

It's not enough to have a good knowledge of Christ, attend church regularly, or even appear to live a Christian life. Christ wants you to make a conscious effort to follow His teachings and mirror His character.

Six

A DISCIPLE IS OBEDIENT

> *Here is the conclusion of the matter: Fear God and obey all His commandments, for this is the whole duty of all humankind.*
>
> **Ecclesiastes 12:13**

Sincere and devout followers of Christ can be distinguished not only by their intellectual understanding of Him but also by their steadfast dedication and adherence to His teachings and principles. It is not enough to possess knowledge about Christ; we must strive to embody His character and follow His teachings with unwavering loyalty. This requires a committed effort to integrate His teachings into your daily life, to become more Christ-like in thought, word, and deed. Being a disciple of Christ demands that we align our actions with God's will. It also involves obeying His commands. Obedience is not only a demonstration of our love for God but also helps us grow in our faith and become more like Christ.

Obedience requires us to submit to God's will, as revealed in His Word, to follow His commands, and to surrender our desires and priorities to Him. In John 14:15, Jesus emphasizes the importance of obedience, stating that if we love Him, we must keep His commands. As we obey God, we understand His character, ways, and plans for our lives. This understanding transforms our hearts and minds, shaping our desires, attitudes, and actions to reflect His will. As we grow in obedience, we grow in our love for God, deepen our faith, and become more like Christ, reflecting His character and glory to the world around us.

As simple as it may sound, obedience brings blessings, and disobedience brings curses. For this reason alone, it is better to adhere to the rules and expectations rather than make mistakes and later try to make up for them through sacrifice (1 Sam 15:22). Humans possess the precious gift of free will—the ability to choose between right and wrong, obedience and disobedience, and the decision to heed the call of discipleship or not. These choices are universal and affect all individuals regardless of identity or location.

When we obey, we open ourselves to a wealth of blessings and positive outcomes. Conversely, choosing to disobey leads to negative consequences that can negate any blessings that may have been bestowed upon us by God, who rewards both good and evil. This concept is demonstrated in Sir Isaac Newton's third law of motion, which states that "every action has an equal and opposite reaction."[1] Disregarding the laws set by God, our parents, or those in authority over us can result in significant repercussions that may leave a lasting impact on our future. The consequences can range from mild to severe, potentially altering the course of our lives. Therefore, we must understand the gravity of our actions and the potential implications before disobeying the rules that govern us, especially the Word of God.

As a minister originally from Africa, I have had the great privilege of living in several countries and various states in America.
This has exposed me to diverse cultures, beliefs, and ways of life.
Through my spiritual journey, I have come to understand the Holy
Scriptures, primarily through the Old Testament teachings of Dr.
Brad Embry, that "God is not a God of location, but a God of the
people." This fundamental truth has shaped my perception of God's
love and grace toward humanity, regardless of where we are or
where we come from. The concept of God's election of Israel has
played a significant role in my spiritual pilgrimage, as it does in the
Hebrew Bible. The idea that God chooses some people over others
has been controversial and over-debated. Still, through the teachings of Walter Moberly in his book The *Old Testament Theology*, I
have gained a profound understanding of its significance. Moberly
emphasizes that "the election of Israel expresses YHWH's love for
Israel.

Moreover, that election is the vocation to serve God to bring
blessings to others." This means that God chose Israel to be a blessing to the world, and this same principle also applies to us. The
instrumental understanding of Israel's election, as seen in Genesis
12:3, answers the question, "Why am I called to discipleship?" My
calling from God was instrumental, like that of Israel. As believers,
we are called to be vessels of God's love and blessings to others.
Our calling is not merely instrumental but a divine mandate to be
a conduit of God's grace to the world. We are not chosen for our
own sake but to serve others and improve their lives. Therefore,
our election is not just about ourselves; it is about serving others
and being a blessing to them. This is the essence of discipleship and
our calling as believers in Christ.

The Bible emphasizes that God desires total obedience from us.
However, history has demonstrated that obedience is a challenging

task for humans. Nevertheless, disobedience always leads to terrible consequences. For example, Adam and Eve lost their home in the Garden of Eden when they disobeyed God. Noah and his family were also the only survivors of the Flood. The Israelites went into exile and captivity several times due to disobedience, and Saul lost his kingship because he refused to obey God.

The prophet Samuel emphasized the importance of obedience when he said to King Saul, "Does the Lord delight in burnt offerings and sacrifices as much as in obeying the Lord? To obey is better than sacrifice, and to heed is better than the fat of rams" (1 Sam 15:22). This statement affirms that obedience to God is more important than any other form of worship. The Bible is our manual for daily living, and we must trust and obey God in every aspect of our lives. It helps us avoid falling into the repeated pattern of disobedience, punishment, and redemption, as seen throughout the Old Testament times. We must learn from the story of Saul's rejection as king (1 Sam 13—15) that a leader's initial success does not guarantee long-term success. A leader's fundamental and worst characteristics always manifest through the test of patience and obedience to God. It is not unusual for every individual chosen by God to undergo the test of obedience, and none of us are exempted from this trial.

Furthermore, obedience to God is indispensable to our relationship with Him. We must strive to obey God in every aspect of our lives, as it is the key to a successful and fulfilling life. Obedience influences the quality of missional discipleship. As we obey God's Word, the Holy Spirit continues to conform us to Christ's image.[2] The trait of complete obedience was exemplified perfectly by Jesus Christ, who not only submitted Himself to His Father's will but also paid the ultimate price by sacrificing His life on the cross (Phil 2:8). Throughout His earthly ministry, Jesus consistently emphasized that He was doing the work that His Father had commissioned Him to do. Jesus's incarnation itself was an act of obedience.

Christ wants us to pursue the same level of obedience. Theologians Halter and Smay argue that a true disciple of Jesus strives to live a heartfelt love and absolute obedience to the Father, even when it demands sacrificing everything for the greater purposes of God's kingdom.[3] Discipleship is a lifelong process that requires a primary response of obedience. When someone claims to be a disciple of Christ, it means they are learning to obey God, His Word, and everything that Jesus taught and commanded.

Christian spiritual formation in the missional movement is becoming more like Christ by conforming to His example through continuous obedience. It involves learning about Christ and living in a way that reflects His character and teachings. This process requires dedication, discipline, and a willingness to be transformed by the Holy Spirit. To be a disciple of Christ, we must prioritize obedience to God's will above all else. This means following God's commands, seeking His guidance, and trusting Him to lead the way. Doing so makes us more like Christ and better equipped to serve Him and others.[4]

A gospel of grace that omits the teaching or practice of complete obedience is not Christ-centered. Discipleship that omits obedience, entirely or partially, is not cross-centered. Without obedience, discipleship is incomplete. Every aspect of following Christ requires complete obedience. In fact, complete obedience is fundamental to God, and everything else, including sacrifice, is derivative of this initial obedience (1 Sam 15:22–23). Sacrifice should flow out of obedience, not vice versa. Any sacrifice that does not come from complete obedience is disobedience and is unpleasant to God. As disciples, we need to obey Christ, the source of eternal salvation to all who follow Him (Heb 5:9). The significance of obedience is evident in both the Old and New Testaments.

Our union with Jesus is based on complete obedience through faith, by which we identify with and become disciples of Christ. It is through our obedience that we carry out His mission. To fulfill the mission in Matthew 28:19–20, we must obey the commandment before teaching it to others. As disciples, His mission is our mission. Therefore, the next chapter focuses on the universal nature of God's mission. The inclusive nature of God's love and His grand mission mandates the calling and equipping of true discipleship.

Ecclesiastes, a book of wisdom literature in the Old Testament, concludes by saying, "Have reverence for God and obey His commands, because this is all that we were created for" (Ecc 12:13). If God created us to glorify Him through obedience, then we must never see it as a burden. Instead, we must see it as the first step in following Christ after receiving Him as our Lord and Savior.

How Can A Disciple Learn And Practice Obedience?

> *Surely, obeying is better than sacrifice . . .*
>
> 1 Samuel 15:22

Learning and practicing obedience involves surrendering to God's will and aligning our lives with His teachings. Here are some ways to learn and practice obedience.

Study and Meditate on God's Word

The Bible is the primary source of God's revelation and instruction, providing us with a clear understanding of His character, will, and commands. By immersing ourselves in God's Word, we can gain deeper insights into His plan for us and the world. Through this knowledge and understanding, we can build a strong foundation for a life of obedience to God.

Cultivate a Heart of Humility

To be obedient, you must cultivate a heart of humility. This means recognizing and accepting your dependence on God and acknowledging His authority over your life. You should approach Him humbly, surrendering your desires, plans, and ambitions to His will. Only then can you be obedient to His commands.

Practice Self-Discipline

Cultivating self-discipline is crucial for obedience and requires much self-control. One way to achieve self-discipline is by engaging in spiritual disciplines such as prayer, fasting, reading the Scriptures, and being accountable to others. Prayer helps us focus on God and His will for our lives. Fasting helps us master our desires and impulses. Reading the Bible provides wisdom and guidance. Being accountable to others helps us to stay on track and avoid distractions. For accountability and community, surround yourself with fellow believers who can provide support and encouragement. Share your struggles and victories with them, and invite them to hold you accountable to living in obedience to God. Practicing these disciplines allows us to resist temptation and continually align ourselves with God's will.

Trust in God's Promises

Trusting in God's promises means you have complete faith in God's commands and instructions, knowing they are for your good. Even when obedience is complex or goes against your natural inclinations, trust in God's sovereignty and believe His ways are higher and better than ours. God's promises are not mere words but a covenant between us and Him. When we trust in His promises, we put our faith in His character, knowing He is faithful and true to His word.

As you lean on God's promises, you will experience His guidance and provision. You can take comfort in knowing that God is always with you, guiding you every step of the way. Even during times of doubt or confusion, you can trust God's promises to give you strength and clarity. Ultimately, trusting in God's promises declares your faith in Him. It's a way of saying that you believe in His goodness and are willing to surrender to His will. When you trust God's promises, you will experience His grace and mercy, changing your life forever.

Act in Faith

Obedience requires us to step out in faith and trust the Lord's guidance and empowerment. As noted in the book of James, "faith without works is dead" (Jas 2:26). This means that we must not only believe in God's promises but also demonstrate our faith through our actions. When we face uncertainties or challenges, trusting God's plan for our lives can be difficult. However, the Bible reminds us that our faith in Christ is what guides us, not what we see or perceive. (2 Cor 5:7). It's easy to get discouraged when things are not going as planned, but staying positive and trusting God can empower us to overcome any obstacle. By acting in faith, we demonstrate our belief in God's ability to lead us through even the most difficult situations.

Obedience is not just about following rules; it's about allowing God to work through our obedience to accomplish His will in our lives and the lives of others. Proverbs 3:5–6 teaches us to trust God completely and not rely on our understanding. We should submit to Him in all our ways, and He will guide us on straight paths. So, whether you're facing a difficult decision, a challenging situation, or a simple task, rely on God to guide you. Through obedience, you can let Him lead your journey and accomplish great things for His glory. Remember, obedience is a lifelong obligation, and it involves the big decisions and the small choices we make each day.

Notes

[1] Nancy Hall, "Newton's Laws of Motion" Glenn Research Center, NASA. October 27, 2022, https://www1.grc.nasa.gov/beginners-guide-to-aeronautics/newtons-laws-of-motion.

[2] Lois Y. Barrett, *Treasure in Clay Jars: Patterns in Missional Faithfulness* (Grand Rapids, MI: Wm. Eerdmans Publishing Co., 2004), 22.

[3] Hugh Halter and Matt Smay, *And: The Gathered and Scattered Church* (Exponential Series) (Grand Rapids, MI: Zondervan, 2010), 120.

[4] Alan Hirsch and Debra Hirsch, *Untamed: Reactivating a Missional Form of Discipleship* (Grand Rapids, MI: Baker Books, 2010), 70.

For Reflection

1. What does obedience mean to you? What role does it play in your life? In what ways have you struggled with it in the past? What caused those struggles?

2. Think of a time when you were obedient even though it was difficult. How did you feel afterward? In what area in your life could you be more obedient? How can you work on improving in that area?

3. What are some benefits of being obedient? What are the consequences of disobedience? How can you practice obedience in your daily life? What steps can you take to make it a habit?

4. Think of a person you admire who is obedient. What qualities do they possess that make them successful in this area?

Food For Thought

As I reflect upon my spiritual journey, I have come to understand that my issues, physical boundaries, and geographical locations do not limit God's love. He takes great pleasure in His people, and this realization enables me to place my complete trust in Him, knowing He cares more about me than I can ever imagine. This truth brings me great comfort and assurance, even when I find myself in unfamiliar places or challenging situations. What about you?

Seven

A DISCIPLE IS MISSIONAL

A disciple's mission is about sharing the message of the cross through words, actions, and attitude and embodying the character of Christ in all ramifications as we inspire others to do the same.

Mission is not about church programs, outreaches, budgets, and faith giving. It is about the salvation of lost people and the needs of the hurting masses. It is about Christ's disciples sharing cross-centered messages through words and actions. Being missional means engaging in God's mission to bring His love, grace, and salvation to the world. This involves adopting a mindset and a lifestyle that reflects God's heart for all people and pursuing avenues to share the good news of Jesus with others. It is about representing His will and provision so that all people can see the truth through us. Living a missional lifestyle means embodying the character and values of Jesus in every aspect of life. It also means seeking to love others as He loved us, to show compassion to those who are hurting, to be generous with our time, talents, and resources, and to extend forgiveness and mercy to those who have wronged us. By living in this way, we become the hands and feet of Jesus in the world, demonstrating His love to those who need it most.

A missional disciple also seeks to build relationships with people who do not yet know Jesus. This involves being present in the community, engaging with people from all walks of life, and creating opportunities to share the gospel with them. It means taking the time to listen to their stories, to understand their struggles, and to offer hope and healing through the power of the gospel. God sends disciples to proclaim His kingdom (Lk 9:1–6; 10:1–12). Christ sent His twelve apostles and then seventy-two others as laborers in a plentiful harvest (Lk 10:2).

Van Gelder and Zscheile propose that discipleship follows Christ into participation in God's mission in the world in the power of the Spirit.[1] As believers are sent to proclaim the message, in most cases, disciples are in danger like sheep among wolves (Lk 10:3) because they announce Christ as the Messiah. This missional engagement is embedded in the life and growth of a disciple. I agree with Maddix when he says, "Discipleship is spiritual formation, Christian nurturing, and mentoring, that includes compassionate service and missional engagement."[2] It is these acts of discipleship that shape people as they grow in grace. Frost and Hirsch also argue that discipleship's essential task is to equip believers to embody the message of Jesus.[3]

The message of Christ they proclaimed is the one that values love, peace (Lk 10:5), and healing (Lk 10:9), which emanate from Christ alone, not riches and power. Missional disciples find their true, God-intended identity as they engage in God's mission with the faith community.[4] Apart from the fact that experience in the mission is an expectation of a missional disciple, missional engagement is also an essential spiritual formation tool. God uses continuous engagement in mission within the faith community to shape and mold disciples. The apostles followed and walked with Jesus. There were lots of people who desired to see what the disciples saw. This is a fragment of God's "gracious will" to His disciples (Lk 10:21). Through the gospel, we also witness the love and power of Christ through His work and His words when He was with His disciples. The arena for God's mission is much bigger now for disciples to be fully missional. We cannot continue to talk about mission without discussing the universal and inclusive nature of God's mission.

The Universal Nature of God's Mission

Most people who read the Bible will acknowledge that the New Testament (NT) strongly emphasizes mission. This is especially the case in the classic Great Commission in Matthew 28:19–20 and is followed through in the book of Acts. It is not often recognized that the mission of Jesus Himself and the mission He entrusted to His followers was shaped and programmed by the nature of God's mission, as seen in the Old Testament. While some works on the theology of mission have paid attention to its Old Testament roots, more academic attention should be paid to the Old Testament roots of God's mission. In light of this, Nicholas Thomas Wright, in his book *Paul: In Fresh Perspective,* argues that down through the centuries, it is fair to say that Christians have been good at a messianic reading of the Old Testament but inadequate (and sometimes utterly blind) at a missional reading of it. Even though authors like Wright,[5] who argue that "mission is a significant key that unlocks the whole grand narrative of the canon of Scripture, came up with something close, a comprehensive OT theology of mission remains to be written.

Few people will accord the Old Testament with little or no missional emphasis. However, the call for the mission mandate and emphasis in the OT cannot be overlooked. If readers are to do justice to the underlying claims and message of the OT, they will see that there is more than just a passing concern that all nations should come to believe in the coming Man of Promise. This is the man who would appear through the seed of the woman Eve, through the family of Shem, and then through the lines of Abraham, Isaac, Jacob, and David.

In light of the above, this chapter centers on the universal nature of God's mission. I have divided it into sections that emphasize God's inclusive nature and mission, as well as some practical guidelines for the Church's participation in the Great Commission, which demands true discipleship.

The Inclusive Nature of God and His Mission

God's character is most clearly depicted in one particular chapter in the Old Testament—Isaiah 45, one of the most notable chapters of the entire Bible. This chapter contains at least eight claims that characterize God's missional nature.

First, Jehovah is the only exclusive God. This is mentioned nine times in Isaiah 45 (see verses 5–6, 14, 18, 21–22). God needs to be proclaimed and worshiped all over the world.

Second, Jehovah is the God of the universe: "the LORD that created the heavens . . . that created the earth and made it" (v. 18). All of the creation manifests the glory of its inventor. His universal lordship and dominion should be announced universally.

Third, Jehovah is the God of the mortal race: "I have made the earth and created man upon it" (v. 12). The entire human race refers to God by creation. This truth must be made known to all people.

Fourth, Jehovah is the God of the sanctimonious order and, therefore, of judgment: "Let the skies pour down righteousness . . . I the LORD have created it" (v. 8). There is one moral system in the world, which is the system established by God. Moreover, God is, therefore, the only judge.

Fifth, Jehovah is the God of chronicles: "Ask me of things to come" (v. 11). "Who hath declared this from ancient time? Have not I the LORD?" (v. 21). God fashions the history of humankind and directs it toward the absolute satisfaction of His disposition. This is the biblical view of history, which lends excellent assistance to world evangelization.

Sixth, Jehovah is the God of revelation: "I have not spoken in secret" (v. 19). God has not left the awareness of Him to the inscrutability of the detailed reasoning of the scholarly but has substantiated it through the prophets for all people.

Seventh, Jehovah is the God of redemption for all people: "Look unto me and be ye saved, all the ends of the earth" (v. 22).

Eighth, Jehovah is the God of all people: "Unto me, every knee shall bow" (v. 23). This is a brief summary of the entirety of the Christian creed.

All of these sweeping claims about God demand global action in evangelism and missions.

OT Passages That Point to the Universal Nature of God's Mission

The Old Testament's message is comprehensive in its expanse and universal in its range. This is evident from the beginning of Genesis 1–11. The creation story in Genesis 1:1–2:4a presents a divine worldview as God creates the universe and everything within it. Genesis 2:4b–25 focuses on the creation of Adam and Eve, the first humans, and their relationship with God and each other. The story of Abraham is central to the Old Testament and has significant implications for understanding the Bible's overall message. When God called Abraham to be His chosen instrument, He gave him the first great commission. This commission was to be the father of all nations. Through Abraham's descendants, all generations would be blessed (Gen 12:2–3).

Abraham's faith journey is an essential part of the Old Testament narrative. He faced many challenges, including leaving his homeland, settling in a foreign land, and waiting to fulfill God's promises. However, he remained faithful to God and became known as the father of the faithful.

The stories of the tower of Babel and the sons of God marrying the daughters of men illustrate the dangers of seeking personal glory and reputation. In both cases, the desire for a name led to failure and judgment from God. In contrast, God granted Abraham a name as a benefit of His grace, and this name was intended to bless others. Abraham's blessing and his becoming a great nation were for the good of all the people on Earth. This is the essence of the mission charge from the very beginning. The following section covers God's calling to Abraham, his journey of faith, and the significance of his story for understanding the Old Testament's overarching message of mission.

God's Call to Abraham

The Bible accounts for the dedicated mission of redeeming the human race carried out by the triune God and His appointed people. The account of the people of Israel is part of the memoir of a grand mission. The record of the corporate sortie of the people of Israel began with the captivating story of a bodily mission—the mission of Abraham. The responsibility of Abraham's mission is stated in God's calling to him: "And I will make of you a great nation, and I will bless you and make your name great so that you will be a blessing. I will bless thee . . . and thou shalt be a blessing . . . and in thee shall all families of the earth be blessed" (Gen. 12:2–3). This is a great commission—the mission of blessing the whole world! Abraham became a great missionary.

God called Abraham, and he acknowledged God's call in faith. He left behind his traditional way of life and embarked on a supernatural errand. Abraham is called the father of faith, but his faith was a means to an end, and that outcome was a mission. Faith by itself lacks content. Faith was expected of Abraham because the carrying out of his mission was usually met with impediments and obstructions, which could be defeated only by faith in God, the originator of the mission.

God's calling to Abraham also carries on to his descendants, as God said to Abraham, "In thy seed shall all the nations of the earth be blessed" (Gen 22:18). The word "seed" as it is used here has a threefold meaning. In the first place, it refers to the people of Israel, for God said to Abraham, "I will multiply thy seed as the stars of the heaven, and as the sand which is upon the seashore" (Gen 22:17). God's intention in establishing the nation of Israel was to show the world through its history His way of salvation and thereby enable all nations to experience His blessings. In the second place, "seed" refers to Jesus Christ. All divine blessings come to us through Jesus Christ, as Paul tells us in the opening verses of his epistle to the Ephesians. In the third place, the word "seed" refers to Christians, whom Paull calls the spiritual children of Abraham (Gal 3:29).

The Apostle Peter clarifies that God calls Christians to the tremendous task of blessing others (1 Pet. 3:9), which is our mission. Christians are missionaries. We cannot be faithful Christians without being missionaries. So, Abraham's mission was passed on to his descendants.

God's call to Abraham was also given to his son, Isaac: "And the LORD appeared unto him [Isaac], and said . . . I will bless thee .

. . and I will perform the oath which I swore unto Abraham, thy father. . . and in thy seed shall all the nations of the earth be blessed" (Gen 26:2–4). It was also given to Jacob: "And, behold, the LORD stood above it and said [to Jacob], I am the LORD God of Abraham, and in thy seed shall all the families of the earth be blessed" (Gen 28:13–14). This thread does not end here. Through the office of Jacob, an inclusive blessing was given to Joseph, who was the next connection in the line of the mission: "Joseph is such a fruitful branch . . . whose boughs run over the wall" (Gen 49:22).

The Missional Message of the Psalms

Repeatedly, the psalmists urge the nations to enter into the praise of the Lord God of Israel. These calls presume that the invitation to accept the gospel had been circulated to the non-Jewish peoples of the world. The key is Psalm 67. God had blessed Israel. He caused His face to shine upon them favorably (an indication of the Aaronic sanctification of Num 6:24–26) so that God's way might be acknowledged worldwide. His salvation among all the nations (Ps 67:2) is apparent. Although one might complain about Psalms 117 and dispute whether it contains a concrete example of missionary teaching, this point cannot be questioned in Psalm 67.

Psalm 67 concludes with the announcement that God blessed Israel precisely so that "all the ends of the earth might fear Him" (Ps 67:7). No less striking are the enthronement or millennial verses in Psalms 93–100. After shifting in successive psalms from an invite to "Sing to the LORD a new song" to a proclamation that "The LORD reigns" (e.g., Psalms 96 and 98 juxtaposed with Psalms 97, 99), the whole series of psalms peaks in Psalms 100 with an invitation for all the nations of the world to come to the Lord with singing and joyous service. Not only should the nations acknowledge their

Creator, but they should also recognize Him as their God and Lord and King above all.

The Missional Teaching of the Prophets

The prophets played a crucial role in communicating God's message to His people about their mission. God used them to provide hints to His people about their purpose, which was to be a blessing to all of creation. Through the prophets' teachings, it is clear that the people of Israel were guided by God and chosen to fulfill a particular mission beyond their boundaries. They were to strive to help all nations understand who God is.

The pedagogy of the prophets offers valuable insights into the nature of missions. The first element is the completeness of God's claim, which emphasizes that God's call to His people is all-encompassing and cannot be ignored. The second element is the totality of God's plan for salvation, which underscores the importance of working toward the salvation of all people. Finally, the third element is the wholeness of the messianic kingdom, which highlights the importance of working toward a complete and perfect world that reflects God's love and justice. Overall, the prophets' teachings provide a powerful reminder of the importance of fulfilling our mission as God's people to work toward a world that reflects God's love, justice, and compassion.

The Missionary Visions of the Prophets

The Old Testament prophetic books offer glimpses of the final consummation of God's plan of redemption through captivating missionary visions. These visions include a "breathtaking image of a sea filled with the water of the knowledge of the glory of God" (Hab 2:14), a heartwarming image of tamed wild beasts living together in peace, "the wolf with the lamb, the leopard with the kid, the calf with the lion" (Is 11:6), a "mouth-watering image of a sumptuous feast on top of the mountain of the Lord" (Is 25:6), and "majestic image of the house of God raised above all mountains with people of all nations flowing to it" (Is 2:2). These four visions represent four precious ideas: 1) the spreading of the knowledge of God's truth to the ends of the earth; 2) the triumph of God's peace and love over hatred and war, leading to a world of harmony; 3) the invitation of all nations to partake in the feast of God's abundant grace; and 4) God's glorious presence in all races. The prophets' inspired ideals will be fulfilled when Jesus returns. However, we have the privilege of carrying out the mission of spreading blessings to the ends of the world before that happens.

OT Elements That Point the Gentiles to God's Mission

That mission to and for the people of the world was the focus is attested to by the representative Gentiles named in the OT text. One need only recall the names of Melchizedek, Jethro, and the mixed multitude of Egyptians who left Egypt with the Israelites, including Balaam, Rahab, Ruth, and the widow at Zarephath. Many others like them also responded through the messages of prophets like Jonah or the major writings of the prophets, who addressed twenty-five chapters of their prophecies to the Gentile nations of their day (e.g., Isa 13–23; Jer 46–51; Ez 25–32). More verses are dedicated to the foreign nations in those twenty-five chapters of the three significant prophets alone than are found in all of the Pauline prison epistles in the NT. There can be little doubt that God was more than mildly interested in winning the nations outside Israel. Israel, in turn, was called to the mission because they had been the objects of God's election. They had been elected to be God's people. However, this was not the Great Commission in the Old Testament.

The Great Commission in the Old Testament was merely an election for the privileged. Still, it was an election for a purpose: the call of one nation to reach all nations. Theologian Edmund Jacob, the author of *Theology of the Old Testament*, agrees that mission is a fundamental concept found throughout the OT.[6] Jacob emphasizes the importance of the book of Jonah in this regard. No less supportive are the voices of Gelin, who says Jonah is "the missionary manual for excellence," and Robert Dobbie, an Old Testament scholar, asserts that Jonah is the best missionary tract ever written.[7] Other scholars allow Isaiah 40–66 to be included in what Johannes Lindblom, the author of *Prophecy in Ancient Israel*, calls the missionary revelations, dealing with the missionary charges (that were) incumbent upon Israel concerning the Gentiles.[8]

Wright claims that although Paul does not quote Old Testament texts in his evangelistic preaching among the Gentiles (as he does when speaking among Jews in synagogues), the content of his message is grounded in and proclaims Israel's monotheistic creational faith.[9] To crown it all, we can see that God makes His servant known as a light to the Gentiles in the OT (Is 42:6; 49:6).

The Influences and Impact of Some Prophetic Messages
In the Life and Ministry of Paul

Saul of Tarsus was a great enemy of the church. However, he was converted on the road to Damascus while persecuting Christians. He became the Apostle Paul—the greatest missionary the church has ever seen. Paul was tasked with explaining the gospel of Christ to the Gentile (non-Jewish) world. Paul also explained the necessity of the two comings of Christ. Dr. Jared W. Ludlow, an associate professor of ancient scripture at Brigham Young University, explains that throughout the New Testament, Jesus, Paul, and others often quoted from Old Testament scripture in their sermons and letters.[10] Quoting from and dialoguing with the OT was a significant background source for writing and compiling God's messages, both to the Jews and the Gentiles. Scripture was also quoted to demonstrate the fulfillment of prophecy. What becomes clear in Paul's ministry is the importance of the gospel message concerning his mission, especially to Gentiles.

The gospel message was so important to Paul that ostracism by others did not matter. Why was this so important? According to 2 Cor 4:3, God promised the gospel right from the beginning through His prophets in the OT scriptures. As seen in Paul's ministry, God's mission was not his invention but the message of God's eternal plan for our redemption. Paul illustrates in several ways that his teachings perfectly harmonize with the OT writings, especially how he dialogues with them. Even after being taught by Jesus for three years, some of His disciples still did not understand how He fulfilled the OT prophecies, but through God's revelation, Paul understood it well.

Practical Guidelines for the Church's Participation in the Great Commission

Some churches do not understand all components of the Great Commission (Matt 28:18–20). No church can claim obedience to the Great Commission until the leadership has "made disciples" by proclaiming the gospel, baptizing, and converting others in the name of the Father, the Son, and the Holy Spirit. This is done to "indoctrinate" converts in the whole counsel of God's Word. God has blessed us with diverse gifts, strengths, offices, and ministries to help us fulfill His grand mission.

Carrying out the Great Commission means evangelizing and making disciples. This should be done with a truth-saturated message (1 Cor 15:1–8), baptizing others with a symbolic ordinance that teaches fundamental doctrines and also teaches them all things, knowledge, and wisdom that incorporate every aspect of their lives. Each baptized convert should be under the discipline and whole-Bible indoctrination of the local church by the Holy Spirit.

For instance, the NT explains how the apostles won converts, baptized them, and nurtured them while organizing them into local churches where they could grow through healthy doctrine and practical edification. The apostles taught them to observe all the biblical ordinances to enhance their spiritual formation. Although evangelizing and communicating with lost people, the reality of salvation is an essential responsibility of the local church. David J. Bosch, a prominent missiologist and theologian, argues in his book *Transforming Mission: Paradigm Shifts in Theology of Mission* that God's mission includes evangelism as one of its critical dimensions,[11] and it is the proclamation of salvation in Christ to those who do not believe in Him.

Even so, the Church must also remind itself that the New Testament emphasizes the feeding (teaching) of those who are already Christians. Indeed, it may be said that the indoctrination of converts in the whole counsel of God's Word is the basic New Testament pattern for world evangelization. The first duty of the Christian body is to understand sound doctrine and implement sound biblical practice. The order of doctrine first, then practice, is both biblical and logical. For example, the Book of Romans contains eleven chapters expounding doctrine, but only the last five discuss practice. Failure to instruct in sound doctrine is the reason for the misconduct and cultural impotence of so many Christians.

One of the primary reasons the Church lacks power in its life is the absence of sound doctrinal truth. We must teach believers that the only effective and efficient way to bring about new life is through God's Word, His chosen method. Moreover, God's method of building the Church determines the means of discipleship and evangelism. Therefore, we must emphasize that Christ is responsible for creating and sustaining the Church through God's Word, as demonstrated throughout the Bible.

To fulfill God's mission, the Church must grow, and this growth is achieved through the proclamation of the gospel and the systematic teaching of the totality of God's Word, including the Old and New Testaments. Therefore, it is essential to emphasize that the Church grows as it teaches and shares the gospel and is strengthened by God's Word. We must recognize the importance of sound doctrinal truth, as it is the foundation of the Church. Only through God's Word can the Church grow and fulfill its mission. The Church must cease being an institution and become a movement that resembles its original form.

An institution is conservative, and a movement is progressive. An institution is more or less passive, yielding to influences from outside. Meanwhile, a movement is active, influencing rather than being influenced. Institutions look to the past and movements to the future. Bosch strengthens this argument by saying that institutions are anxious, while movements are prepared to take risks. Institutions guard boundaries while movements cross them. For the Church to thrive in its missional work, it must remain an active movement.

God didn't choose Israel to obtain the covenantal blessing for itself alone. Israel was designated to share God's blessings with the entire world. Admittedly, with Abraham, and then most decisively with Moses, the spotlight had been set for an entire nation to be connected in a ministry of being priests and witnesses to all people. The treaty that David received was not to be greedily spent on themselves but to be "a covenant for all humankind." Isaiah repeated this point, saying it was to be "a covenant for the people and enlightenment for the Gentiles." This universal mission completes the message and mission of the OT. That is why the first eleven chapters of Genesis focus on all the families and nations of the world before one family is called to serve all the other families.

The Old Testament is a complete image of God's grand mission to every people group in the world. It is the code that unlocks the entire Bible. Just as the prophets, priests, and others were used to project the imagery of God's inclusive mission, true discipleship means obeying the great commission in Matthew 28. That's why it is so paramount to understand the essential characteristics of true discipleship. However, it is not enough to understand the characteristics; we must also ensure that they become a part of our lives as we carry our cross to follow Christ.

Proven Ways to Be a Missional Disciple

Embrace the Great Commission

The Great Commission of Jesus Christ, as mentioned in Matthew 28:19–20, is a call to all believers to go out into the world and make disciples of all nations. This commission is a commandment to share the good news of Jesus Christ with people from all walks of life, regardless of race, religion, or social status. Christians must embrace this commission as a personal calling and look for opportunities to spread the gospel to others.

This can be done in various ways, both locally and globally. Locally, we can reach out to our friends, family members, colleagues, and neighbors and share the hope and love of Jesus Christ. We can also volunteer in our churches, participate in outreach programs, and support missions that aim to bring the gospel to people in our communities.

On a global scale, countless opportunities exist to share the gospel with people from different cultures and backgrounds. This can be done through short-term mission trips, supporting and partnering with missionaries and organizations dedicated to spreading the gospel, and even through the use of technology and social media, which allow us to connect with people from all over the world. By fulfilling Jesus Christ's Great Commission, we can help bring salvation and hope to those who need it most and positively impact the world around us.

Live as an Example

This means being intentional about every aspect of your life, reflecting the character and teachings of Jesus. It's not just about attending church services or holding a Bible; it means embodying the principles of love, kindness, humility, and generosity in your daily interactions with people. Let your actions, attitudes, and relationships be a testimony to the transformative power of Jesus Christ. People should see the difference in how you treat others, speak, and handle situations. Your life should be an example of the positive change that comes from following Jesus.

Living as an example does not mean living a perfect life but acknowledging your flaws and striving toward growth and improvement. Your mistakes should be a learning opportunity, and your successes should be celebrated with humility. Living as an example makes you a light in the world. Others will see Christ in you and be drawn to Him through your lifestyle.

Build Relationships

One of the most crucial aspects of spreading the gospel is building solid, meaningful relationships with individuals in your community and social circles. To do this, you must show genuine care, compassion, and interest in their lives. Be an attentive listener, seeking to understand and empathize with other people's perspectives. As you build these authentic connections, demonstrate love and acceptance, which can create opportunities to share your faith and make disciples. Remember, relationships take time and effort to develop but can bring substantial rewards.

Share Your Faith

Sharing your faith can be a powerful way to positively impact those around you. By opening up about your personal experiences and beliefs, you can create meaningful connections with others and inspire them to consider their spiritual journey. To share your faith effectively, be sensitive to the Holy Spirit's leading and consider the unique needs and perspectives of those you speak with. You can share your story and the gospel message through personal conversations, extending invitations to church or Christian events, or using social media to spread uplifting messages of hope and love.

Serve Others

Serving others is a constructive and powerful way to put love into action. It involves seeking opportunities to meet the needs of those around us, and it can be done through small acts of kindness or more significant acts of service. By serving others, we demonstrate God's love and compassion for all of us, regardless of our differences. This can be incredibly constructive in a world that often values individualism and self-interest over community and collaboration.

To serve others, we must go beyond our interests and desires and consider other people's needs. This means being willing to listen, empathize, and take action when we see an opportunity to help. Serving others is not a one-time act but a lifestyle that requires consistent effort. The Bible provides many examples of serving others, and these examples can inspire us to do the same. For instance, Matthew 25:35–40 speaks to the importance of serving others, and this passage reminds us that by serving those in need, we are serving Jesus Himself. Galatians 5:13–14 emphasizes the importance of using our liberty to benefit others in love and to love our neighbor as ourselves.

Serving others is not always easy, and it can mandate us to stroll beyond our comfort zone or our perceived limits. However, through our acts of service, we can provide tangible examples of how God's love can make a difference in the world. We can motivate others to follow in our footsteps and initiate a wave of kindness and compassion that outstretches far beyond our close circle of influence. Ultimately, serving others is a constructive way to live out our faith and fulfill God's mission for our lives.

Support Missions

There are various ways in which you can support gospel missions and participate in spreading God's Word both locally and globally. One most straightforward way is praying for missionaries, asking for God's guidance and strength to be with them. Additionally, you can offer financial support to mission organizations that work toward this cause. Your financial contribution can help fund the resources used to spread the gospel. Finally, you can immerse yourself in the mission by going on short-term trips, which offer a unique opportunity to experience different cultures and connect with the people you serve.

Stay Rooted in Prayer

Developing a vibrant prayer life is paramount for remaining rooted in God. It is also paramount to be effective in missional activities. Prayer is not just a one-way communication where we ask God for things but also a two-way conversation where we listen to God's guidance and direction. When we pray, we invite God to lead us, give us wisdom, and empower us to engage in His mission. Christ modeled the significance of prayer in His own life and ministry. In Mark 1:35, we see Jesus getting up early to pray. In Luke 6:12, we see Him praying the entire night before choosing His twelve disciples. In Matthew 6:9–13, Jesus teaches His disciples the Lord's Prayer, a model for how to pray and stay connected to God. Prayer is also crucial for being missional.

As we engage in God's mission, we will encounter various challenges, obstacles, and opportunities. Prayer helps us to stay focused on God's will and to seek His guidance in navigating these situations. We can pray for the lost, opportunities to share the gospel, and the advancement of God's kingdom. In Colossians 4:2–4, Paul urges the Colossians to dedicate themselves to prayer, be watchful and thankful, and pray for open doors for the gospel to be proclaimed. By participating in God's mission and staying rooted in prayer, we join Him in His work of redemption, restoration, and transformation in the lives of individuals and communities. We can trust that God will guide and empower us to be effective witnesses for Him. So, let us stay rooted in prayer and engage with the world around us, seeking to bring the love and message of Jesus to those who have yet to experience it.

Notes

[1] Craig Van Gelder and Dwight J. Zscheile, *The Missional Church in Perspective: Mapping Trends and Shaping the Conversation* (Grand Rapids, MI: Baker Academic, 2011), 89.

[2] Mark A. Maddix, *Missional Discipleship: Partners in God's Redemptive Mission* (Kansas City, MO: Beacon Hill Press, 2013), 29.

[3] Michael Frost and Alan Hirsch, *The Shaping of Things to Come: Innovation and Mission for the 21st-Century Church*, (Ada, MI: Baker Books, 2003).

[4] Beard, 185.

[5] Nicholas Thomas Wright, *Paul: In Fresh Perspective* (Minneapolis: Fortress Press, 2005).

[6] Edmond Jacob, *Theology of the Old Testament* (London: Hodder & Stoughton, 1958).

[7] Robert Dobbie, *Canadian Journal of Theology: A Quarterly of Christian Thought* Vols 1 - 16 (1955 - 1970)," Biblical Studies.Org.UK, July 1958, https://biblicalstudies.org.uk/articles_canadian-journal.php.

[8] Johannes Lindblom, *Prophecy in Ancient Israel* (Augsburg Fortress Publishing, 1962).

[9] Nicholas Thomas Wright, *Paul: In Fresh Perspective* (Fortress Press, 2005).

[10] Jared W. Ludlow, "Paul's Use of Old Testament Scripture," in *How the New Testament Came to Be*, Brigham Young University Religious Education Center, 2006, https://rsc.byu.edu/how-new-testament-came-be/pauls-use-old-testament-scripture.

[11] David J. Bosch, *Transforming Mission: Paradigm Shifts in Theology of Mission* (Maryknoll, NY: Orbis Books, 2011).

For Reflection

1. How do you define being "missional" as Christ's disciple? In what ways have you shared your faith with others recently?

2. How does being missional impact your relationships with people with different beliefs or values? In what ways can you incorporate mission into your daily life and interactions with others?

3. In what ways do you feel called to share Christ's love with others? What fears or obstacles keep you from doing so?

4. How do you measure your effectiveness in being a missional disciple? What changes can you make to be more impactful?

5. Who are some individuals you could invest in and disciple toward a missional lifestyle?

Food For Thought

The ultimate mark of a disciple is not the number of people they have led to Christ, but in the quality of leaders, they have raised to continue the mission. It is not about personal achievement but about empowering and guiding others to become leaders who positively impact this world as they lead people to Christ.

Eight

A DISCIPLE IS A MULTIPLIER

> *When you produce much fruit, you are my true disciples. This brings great glory to my Father.*
>
> **John 15:8**

Becoming a disciple of Christ involves more than just personal spiritual development. It also includes sharing the good news of salvation with others and helping them to grow in their faith. This process of multiplication lies at the heart of discipleship. Creating more disciples spreads the gospel's message further, and more people are welcomed into God's family. For us to carry out this process faithfully, God has divulged a distinct plan in the Holy Scripture. Multiplication is a fundamental and indispensable standard of all growth in the physical world. Multiplication does not occur by just adding one unit to another but by multiplying. God's grand plan of reaching the world is similar in the spiritual realm.

Discipleship always starts with a call to be fishers for men and women for the kingdom. The decision by those called is the first critical step of true discipleship. Converts must develop beyond their decision to become responsible and reproductive followers of Christ who possess the ability to raise and nurture other new believers. Let's face it: winning new converts is very important for the Body of Christ, but raising and nurturing them to follow Jesus and become spiritually multiplicative is equally imperative. Whenever you win a convert and are blessed to train them, that one convert will then convert others, training and equipping them to reach others. This is the nature of God's mission. Notice that Jesus did not just call only one disciple in the gospel accounts; He called twelve, trained them, and then charged them to multiply. The disciples took their cue from Jesus and sought to be fruitful and multiply. They were intentional about Jesus's command in Matthew 28:18–20. Disciples fully embrace the leverage from building capacity for disciple-making by multiplying healthy, reproducing churches.[1] Each disciple should have the ability and the characteristics embedded in them to reproduce.

Timothy and the Apostle Paul are great examples of the multiplication principle. Timothy was a young man whom Paul mentored. He joined Paul's missionary team on Paul's second missionary journey, and they traveled extensively throughout the Mediterranean, preaching the gospel and planting churches. Paul not only shared the gospel with those he encountered but also trained and equipped them to continue spreading the message after he moved on to other areas. Paul's letters to the churches he founded show his emphasis on discipleship and the importance of sharing the good news with others.

This approach enabled the gospel to spread throughout the Mediterranean world and beyond, eventually forming the early Christian church. Paul invested deeply in Timothy, helping him to grow in his faith and equipping him for ministry. In his letters to Timothy, Paul shared wisdom and guidance on everything from leadership to character and doctrine. Timothy took these teachings to heart and became a respected leader in the early church. Timothy's impact didn't stop there. Paul encouraged him to continue multiplying disciples by training others to do ministry work.

In 2 Timothy 2:2, Paul instructs Timothy to entrust the teachings he has heard him share to reliable individuals in the presence of many witnesses. He says these entrusted individuals should also possess the necessary qualities to teach others. Paul recapped this plan in his letter to Timothy: "And the things that thou hast heard of me among many witnesses, the same commit thou to faithful men, who shall be able to teach others also" (2 Tim 2:2). Through this divine plan of multiplication, the gospel would spread worldwide. This passage emphasizes the importance of mentorship, discipleship, and passing knowledge on to future generations. Timothy took this charge seriously. His commitment to multiplying disciples helped spread the gospel throughout the ancient world.

A more recent example of a disciple who was a multiplier is William Carey, a British missionary who is considered the father of modern missions. Carey went to India in 1793 and spent several decades preaching the gospel there. He also planted churches and translated the Bible into numerous Indian languages. But Carey didn't stop there. He also trained Indian pastors and evangelists, equipping them to carry on the work of spreading the gospel in their communities. Carey's emphasis on multiplication was revolutionary for his time, as many other missionaries saw their work as primarily focused on converting individuals rather than creating a self-sustaining movement. But Carey saw the value in investing in local leaders who could continue the work long after he was gone. His approach was highly successful, and today, millions of Indian Christians can trace their spiritual heritage back to Carey's work.

Hudson Taylor is another notable example of a disciple that we should emulate. He was a British missionary who spent over fifty years in China during the nineteenth century. Taylor's approach to mission work was unique and highly effective. He learned the Chinese language and culture, dressed like a Chinese man, and made efforts to contextualize the gospel message to the Chinese people. But Taylor's impact went beyond his personal ministry efforts. He founded the China Inland Mission (now known as OMF International), an organization dedicated to training and sending out missionaries to share the gospel in China. Taylor recognized the importance of equipping and empowering others to do ministry, and his approach led to the creation of a strong network of missionaries who continued his work long after his death. Today, over 16,000 churches in China can trace their roots back to the work of Taylor and the China Inland Mission. Taylor's emphasis on multiplication and his commitment to training and equipping others to do ministry work has impacted the spread of the gospel in China and beyond.

Looking at how Jesus called out His disciples, He chose these men, trained them, disciplined them, equipped them, and sent them forth to reach others. That is how discipleship works. Just like Jesus reached out to His twelve disciples, if a believer reaches to one person, disciple them, and commits them to disciple another, the gospel will spread like wildfire, as seen in the early church. To clarify the objective, I am not telling you to disciple people just enough to build your ministry, church, or denomination. The sole objective of disciplining people is missional; it is to be fishers of men and women for God's kingdom. Fulfilling the Great Commission is not dependent on tricks, secret techniques, and updated technology, as you may have learned from some so-called preachers. The Great Commission first depends on the Holy Spirit working through the maturity of committed disciples.

The only hope for the growth of the Christian faith is multiplication. Although not as fast as other secular movements, multiplication gradually becomes the fuel that grows the Church for future generations.[2] For example, one of Jesus's first disciples, Andrew, shared the gospel with Peter, his brother. Peter shared the gospel with others who later became reproductive. Believers scattered from Jerusalem continued to spread the gospel. Everyone they reached multiplied, and the reproductive process continued. Another example is Ananias. God used him to raise Paul in his Christian journey.

Paul trained disciples and committed Timothy while he was training others. Timothy instructed faithful men who would teach others. Faithful men grew and discipled others, continuing the multiplication process. Each disciple, as a multiplier in the network, continued to multiply. Spiritual multiplication can be a complex concept to grasp. However, at its core, it is all about becoming a devotee of Christ and following in His footsteps. By doing so, we can carry out His work as He intended. To put it simply, being a disciple means not only believing in Christ but also embodying His teachings and values. It involves committing to continuous learning, growth, and service to others. Jesus emphasized the importance of producing abundant fruit as a sign of true discipleship (Col 1:10). We must strive to impact the world around us and help others grow in their faith. Through our efforts, we can bring glory to our Father and inspire others to follow in our footsteps. By being true disciples and following Christ's example, we can make a tangible difference in the world and help spread His message of love and compassion.

Proven Ways to Be a Multiplier

As a disciple, being a multiplier involves taking a role in the lives of others by investing time and effort into equipping and empowering them to become disciples. It means building relationships and providing guidance, support, and resources to help others grow spiritually and mature in their faith. Through this process, disciples become catalysts for change and transformation in the lives of those around them, multiplying the impact of their discipleship journey. Here are some proven ways that disciples can become multipliers.

Intentional Discipleship

Intentional discipleship is a deliberate approach to nurturing spiritual growth in yourself and others. It involves seeking out individuals eager to learn and grow in their faith and walking alongside them. This process requires sharing your knowledge, experiences, and insights to help them develop a strong foundation in their relationship with God. Discipleship is not a one-size-fits-all approach. Intentional discipleship recognizes this by creating a personalized approach that helps individuals grow according to their unique needs. This involves equipping them to follow Jesus wholeheartedly and deeply understand His teachings, values, and principles. Intentional discipleship is a rewarding journey that demands commitment, patience, and a willingness to learn from others. It is a process that transforms not only the individuals involved but also the community at large.

Be an Example

Be an example of a committed and mature disciple. Your words, actions, and attitudes should demonstrate Christ's character and values. Live a life that others can emulate and aspire to. Your example will speak volumes and inspire others to follow Jesus.

Share Knowledge and Teach

Share biblical truths and teachings with others. Provide opportunities for Bible study, small group discussions, and/or one-on-one mentoring. Your aim should be to help others understand and apply God's Word to their lives and equip them with the knowledge and understanding they need to grow in their faith. By sharing knowledge, you can help others deepen their relationship with God and enhance their spiritual growth.

Encourage Spiritual Practices

Help others develop spiritual disciplines that will enhance their spiritual growth. These include prayer, Bible reading, and worship. By providing guidance and support, you can help them establish a consistent and vibrant spiritual life that will enable them to connect with their inner self and the Lord. Inspire them to explore diverse spiritual practices and find what works for them, as every individual's spiritual journey is unique.

Empower and Release

Mentoring is an empowering journey that requires recognizing and appreciating the diverse gifts, talents, and abilities of the individuals under your guidance. Each person has unique strengths that can be utilized to serve others and God's kingdom. Encouraging the use of these gifts is vital to the development of the mentee as well as the success of the mission. As you mentor disciples, provide opportunities for them to exercise their leadership skills and take on responsibilities that align with their abilities. This can involve delegating tasks that allow them to make meaningful contributions to the team. Create opportunities for them to serve in various capacities, such as community outreach programs or church activities. This will allow them to experience different roles and find their niche.

Provide a safe and supportive environment that allows your mentee to grow and learn from experience. Giving them room to make mistakes is essential to their development. Instead of criticizing them when they make mistakes, provide constructive feedback that helps them learn. As they progress, celebrate their achievements and encourage them to strive for excellence. By empowering and releasing young disciples in the faith, you are equipping them to reach their full potential while contributing to the growth of God's kingdom.

Challenge and Stretch

As you disciple others, challenge them to stretch beyond their comfort zones. This means encouraging them to step out in faith, take risks, and try things that may feel uncomfortable or unfamiliar. When we push ourselves beyond what is easy and safe, we often discover new strengths and abilities that we didn't know we had.

One way to stretch those you disciple is to challenge them to reach out to others. This could mean initiating conversations about faith, sharing their testimony, or inviting someone to church. By stepping out this way, they can help others come to know Christ and experience His love. Engaging in acts of service and love is another meaningful way to stretch and challenge your disciples. Please encourage them to seek ways to serve others in their community, whether by volunteering at a homeless shelter, visiting the sick, or helping with a community event. When we serve others, we reflect the heart of Christ and demonstrate His love to those around us.

Above all, help those you disciple develop a mindset of obedience and a passion for advancing God's kingdom. This means teaching them to listen to the Holy Spirit's voice and follow His leading, even when it is uncomfortable. By keeping their eyes fixed on Jesus and

His mission, they can make a lasting impact on the world and bring glory to God.

Pray For and With Others

As a mentor and disciple-maker, you should prioritize prayer for those under your guidance. Interceding on their behalf, lifting them in prayer, and seeking God's guidance, protection, and provision are paramount. Also, pray for their spiritual growth so that they will grow deeper in their faith and their understanding of God's Word. You should also pray for their relationships, that they will have healthy interactions with others and build strong, God-honoring connections. Furthermore, pray for their struggles and challenges, knowing God is the ultimate source of comfort and strength. Create opportunities to pray together, spontaneously or when needed, building a culture of dependence on God.

As you pray with your mentees, you'll find that your relationship with each other and God deepens. Praying together fosters a sense of community and trust, a powerful reminder that we are not alone in our faith journey. Being a multiplier requires a genuine investment of time, energy, and love in the lives of others. It involves a commitment to walking alongside them, supporting their growth, and empowering them to become disciple-makers. By multiplying disciples, you contribute to expanding God's kingdom as the gospel impacts and transforms more people.

Mission and Multiplication Growth Plan

Although we all need growth in all areas, we should prayerfully assess our areas of strength and weakness. This is one way to discover areas that need more attention. In his book, *Spiritual Disciplines for the Christian Life,* Donald S. Whitney, a professor of biblical spirituality and associate dean at Southern Baptist Theological

Seminary, explains that it is disobedience to Christ's command to spread His message when we don't allow evangelism to be a natural overflow of our Christian life.[3] He also believes we can find long-term solutions to our inconsistency and frequent lack of witnessing if we discipline ourselves for evangelism.[4] Since mission and multiplication go together, we can utilize a single plan to help us grow in both areas.

Second Timothy 3:16–17 says that all Scripture is God-breathed and is useful for teaching, rebuking, correcting, and training in righteousness so that we can be thoroughly equipped for His mission. So, we must let the Word confront our selfishness, pride, anger, and speech. The Word of God will groom and mature us in all aspects of our life and spiritual formation. We must allow the Word to train, correct, keep, and guide us on the righteous path as we live in this wicked world. In this way, through the Word, we can minister Christ to others as it has ministered to us. We should eliminate any sin that makes our words sound hollow. While attempting to do that, we must also be convinced that we cannot delay our witnessing until we reach sinless perfection.[5] How are we to do that? A Christian mission and multiplication growth plan involves developing a strategic approach to fulfill the Great Commission and multiply disciples. Here are some pivotal elements to weigh when forming such a plan.

Vision and Mission

Defining the vision and mission of your church or ministry is a critical step in ensuring the effectiveness and success of your outreach efforts. Consider and articulate your specific purpose and calling when reaching the lost and making disciples. What values and beliefs guide your actions, and how do they inform your approach to ministry? What are the goals you hope to achieve, both short-term and long-term? By responding to these inquiries, you can generate a comprehensive and inspiring vision that will motivate and guide your team in their efforts to herald the gospel and positively impact the lives of those around you.

Prayer and Seeking God's Guidance

Start your mission and multiplication efforts with prayer. Seek God's guidance, direction, and discernment as you develop and implement your plan. Rely on the Holy Spirit for wisdom, insight, and empowerment, knowing that the success of your efforts ultimately depends on His guidance and provision. Take time to connect with God and listen to His voice, as He will provide you with the clarity, inspiration, and strength you need to carry out your mission with excellence. Prayer should not just be a ritual but an influential tool that can transform your vision, strategy, and outcomes.

Leadership Development

Investing in the development of leaders passionate about mission and multiplication is crucial for the growth and success of any organization. To achieve this, comprehensive training, mentorship, and resources should be provided to help these leaders enhance their understanding of discipleship and equip them with the skills to lead and reproduce disciples effectively. Leadership development programs should be designed to meet each leader's specific needs, considering their strengths, weaknesses, and areas of interest. These programs can include workshops, seminars, coaching, mentoring, and access to relevant resources, such as books, podcasts, and online courses.

Through these programs, leaders can better understand their leadership style, learn effective communication and decision-making skills, and develop strategies for building and leading successful teams. They can also learn how to identify and develop potential leaders within their organization, creating a sustainable pipeline of leaders for the future. Investing in leadership development not only benefits individual leaders but also has a positive impact on the blossoming and triumph of the organization. Faith communities can attract and maintain top talent and execute their mission and vision by forming a culture of ongoing learning and maturation.

Discipleship Pathway

Establish a clear discipleship pathway that outlines the steps to ensure a structured and effective process for growth and development. This pathway should define the various stages of discipleship and provide necessary resources, curriculum, and mentoring opportunities to support individuals at each stage. The ultimate goal of this pathway should be the multiplication of disciples who are equipped and empowered to make more disciples.

Outreach and Evangelism Strategies

Sharing the gospel is a fundamental part of the Christian faith. To do this effectively, develop strategies that are detailed and well-planned. This involves identifying specific target groups or communities that are most receptive to the message and customizing evangelistic initiatives that are relevant and engaging to them. One way to reach out to these groups is to create programs that cater to their unique needs and interests. For instance, if the target group comprises young adults, hosting events or workshops that address relevant topics such as careers, relationships, or mental health is a great way to start meaningful conversations and build relationships. Similarly, if the target community is a specific ethnic group, providing resources and materials tailored to their culture and language can help make the message more accessible and relatable.

In addition, your strategies should be able to help believers with the necessary skills and resources to share their faith effectively. This could also involve providing training on how to initiate and sustain conversations, how to answer difficult questions, and how to share personal testimonies. By doing so, we can empower believers to engage in more meaningful and fruitful dialogues with others. Ultimately, the goal is to design a welcoming and inclusive community that is open to the message of salvation. By developing detailed strategies, we can help to break down barriers and share Christ's love with those who need it most.

Small Group and Community Engagement

Encourage the formation of small groups or discipleship communities where individuals can grow spiritually, build relationships, and be accountable to one another. Create an atmosphere of love, support, and discipleship within these groups. Emphasize the significance of multiplication, motivating group members to reproduce and initiate new groups.

Missions Mobilization

We must take a deliberate approach to equipping and mobilizing individuals for local and global mission work. First, we should provide comprehensive training to ensure that those who embark on mission trips are well-prepared to meet the unique challenges they may face. This may include training in cross-cultural communication, evangelism, and practical skills such as healthcare or construction. In addition, we must also provide opportunities for individuals to form partnerships with missionaries and organizations to gain a deeper understanding of the challenges faced by those who work in the mission field. This could involve participating in long-term mission work or acting as a support system for those already serving.

Moreover, we must also encourage participation in community outreach initiatives to develop a deeper understanding of the needs of our local communities and how we can serve them. This could involve partnering with local charities or non-profit organizations and developing our initiatives to meet the needs of those around us. Ultimately, we must cultivate a heart for missions and a global perspective among believers. This can be achieved through regular prayer, Bible study, and teaching on the importance of missions in the life of the Church. As we engage in mission work locally and globally, we gain a deeper appreciation for the diversity of God's creation and our role in spreading the good news to others.

Measurement and Evaluation

To ensure the success of your mission and multiplication efforts, establish a comprehensive measurement and evaluation system. This system should include a wide range of metrics and evaluation tools, such as surveys, feedback forms, and performance indicators designed to track progress and assess effectiveness. To ensure you are obtaining accurate information, reevaluate and scrutinize the data obtained through this system regularly. By doing so, you can pinpoint maturation areas and identify opportunities for refinement. For example, if you notice a drop in performance indicators, you may need to adjust your strategy or allocate additional resources. Celebrating triumphs is also a crucial part of the measurement and evaluation process. Recognizing and rewarding the team's successes can motivate and engage them and build a positive and supportive team culture.

In addition to analyzing the data obtained through your measurement and evaluation system, gather feedback from ministry leaders and members, converts, those in the discipleship program, and supporting partners. This feedback can give you some helpful insights into the efficacy of your mission and can help you identify areas for improvement. Overall, establishing a comprehensive system of measurement and evaluation and analyzing and scrutinizing the data obtained through this system is essential for making meaningful progress toward your goals.

Continuous Training and Support

Provide continuous training, resources, and support to individuals dedicated to mission and multiplication. The objective is to help them improve their skills and knowledge in their respective fields, become better leaders, and multiply their impact in their work or ministry. To achieve this goal, offer a range of discipleship training programs, leadership development initiatives, and mentorship opportunities. These programs should focus on developing the core values, principles, and practices essential for success in mission and multiplication.

Discipleship training should provide a strong foundation for individuals to grow in their faith and develop a deeper understanding of the Christian worldview. Leadership development programs should focus on cultivating the skills and qualities required to lead effectively. Mentorship programs should provide opportunities for individuals to receive guidance, support, and feedback from experienced leaders who have already succeeded in their respective fields. By providing ongoing training, resources, and support, individuals involved in mission and multiplication can continue to learn and grow to become influential in their lives, work, and ministry.

Celebration and Accountability

Acknowledge and celebrate the positive impact of transformational experiences such as salvation and discipleship multiplication. At the same time, create a culture of accountability where individuals and groups can share their progress and challenges and seek support and guidance. Doing so ensures that the transformative journey is celebrated, supported, and sustained in the long run. Remember, a mission and multiplication growth plan should be elastic and adaptable to scripturally react to changing contexts and needs. Seek God's guidance, evaluate the effectiveness of your strategies, and make adjustments as necessary to remain faithful to the mission of making disciples who make disciples.

Sample Plan for New Disciples

Joshua 1:8 teaches us a practical way to use the Word of God and be successful. "This Book of the Law (the Holy Scripture) should not depart from our mouth, but we are to constantly meditate on it day and night so that we may be careful to do according to all that is written in the Scripture. For then, we will make your way prosperous, and then we will have good success" (Jos 1:7–8 ESV). Based on the Holy Scriptures, here is a basic sample plan for new disciples.

- This plan starts with first studying the Word of God (the New Testament for now) daily. Study at least one chapter per day, pick a verse in that chapter, memorize it, and use it as your verse of the day.
- Second, as you memorize it, keep that verse in your mouth; say it continuously or repeatedly.
- Third, meditate on it throughout the day. You may want to utilize a study Bible or commentaries during your study and

meditation. Pray for God to reveal something to you through that Scripture. Allow God to minister to you.

- Fourth, be careful to follow through with what God is telling you through His Word for that day.
- Fifth, do not keep it to yourself; share your experience with God with at least one person a day, the same person or people for one week.

In case you're wondering how you will engage people with your holy experience, McClendon and Jared proposed that every venue and every relationship is an opportunity to live out the Christian life before others and to engage them kindly, looking for opportunities to talk to them about your experience with God.[6] This does not mean we will push Jesus to their face; it merely means evangelism will be at the forefront of our minds as we engage with others regardless of the activities. Always pray for every one you share with at the end of the day because prayer is the key here, and interceding for them can turn things around in their life. Journal your experience, verse of the day, areas of growth, and the people you have reached for the next three months.

Exercises one to four should be done repeatedly daily. Exercise five should be done weekly with a different person or persons. If you follow this plan or spiritual exercise closely, you will be amazed at how much growth and maturity you attain. McClendon and Jared encourage us to desire, as the early church did, to engage all the time in all venues in all ways.[7] Whatever we do, our engagement should be natural and not forced.[8] Remember, Jesus only called His disciples; He never forced anyone to follow Him, including you. Following this plan means being intentional about Christ's command in Matthew 28:18–20. It also means we should actively engage in building the capacity to reproduce healthy and faithful believers.

Notes

[1] Todd Wilson, *Multipliers: Leading Beyond Addition* (N.p.: United States Exponential, 2017), 55.

[2] Bob Roberts Jr., *The Multiplying Church: The New Math for Starting New Churches* (Grand Rapids, MI: Zondervan, 2008), 61.

[3] Donald S. Whitney, *Spiritual Disciplines for the Christian Life Study Guide* (Colorado Springs, CO: NavPress Publishing Group, 2014), 50–52.

[4] Ibid.

[5] Ibid, 136.

[6] Adam P. McClendon and Jared E. Lockhart, *Timeless Church: Five Lessons From Acts* (Nashville, TN: B & H Academic, 2020), 107.

[7] Ibid, 106.

[8] Ibid.

For Reflection

1. Have you had the privilege of being someone's disciple? If so, how have you used the knowledge and wisdom you gained to multiply the impact of your own life on others?

2. What qualities must a disciple possess to become a multiplier? How can you cultivate and develop these qualities within yourself?

3. How can you inspire and encourage others to become disciples and multipliers? What actions can you take to help them grow and develop in this area?

4. How important is accountability in the journey of being a disciple and multiplier? How can you find accountability partners who will support and challenge you as you seek to grow in these areas?

5. What steps can you take to become a better disciple and expand your positive influence on others?

Food For Thought

In times like these, it is more important than ever to have a robust support system. Being part of a faith community can make all the difference. When we prioritize fellowship and church meetings, we can encourage each other to stay connected and uplift one another. This creates a nurturing environment where hope and kindness can flourish. Let us work together to build a loving community where Christ reigns and where we can all find hope, comfort, and support.

Nine

A DISCIPLE IS COMMUNAL

Regular fellowship and intentional engagement in a cross-centered community provide the hope, love, and encouragement you need to thrive in your walk with Christ.

Discipleship is a multifaceted concept that varies in application depending on the context and belief system. It encompasses building a sense of community and collective engagement among the disciples. In many spiritual or religious traditions, discipleship involves individuals coming together to learn from and support their spiritual teacher or guide, forming a communal bond based on shared beliefs and practices. It can provide a nurturing and supportive environment for growth, learning, and mutual support among Christians. By being part of a community of like-minded individuals, disciples can share their experiences, ask questions, and seek guidance from their spiritual mentors. This sense of community can also foster a sense of accountability and responsibility toward one another, creating a solid bond beyond simple belief and practice. The missional aspect of discipleship speaks a lot about the missional movement.

The missional movement is a Christian movement that emphasizes the role of discipleship in shaping the mission and purpose of a faith community. According to this perspective, a disciple's characteristics should be the guiding principles that shape how a faith community develops its mission as a spiritual formation effort. This means that a faith community's mission is influenced and shaped by the qualities of its disciples, as they are the ones who carry out the mission. To provide a context for transformative experiences that shape a disciple's identity, the faith community plays a fundamental role.

The community serves as an environment for disciples to practice and embody Christ's teachings as they grow in their faith and spiritual maturity. In this way, the community is ever-present, interactive, formative, and transformative throughout our spiritual formation. As discipleship is not an individualistic endeavor, the faith community's role is integral to the individual's spiritual formation process. The faith community's support, encouragement, and accountability empower disciples to live out their mission and purpose. They are prepared with the knowledge, skillfulness, and resources required to fulfill their calling as they impact the world around them.

In the Bible, we see an example of the missional movement in the life and teachings of Jesus. He called His disciples to follow Him and be fishers of men (Mt 4:19), and through His teachings and guidance, He shaped their mission and purpose. The book of Acts also illustrates how the early Christian community provided a context for transformative experiences that shaped the identity and mission of its members and how the community played a critical role in their spiritual formation.

Discipleship can also help the Church evaluate its faith communities. Faith communities should reflect the life of God's kingdom, as that is how they can continue to fulfill this purpose. This involves evaluating whether the community is living out the characteristics of discipleship and whether it is a context of transformative experiences. If there are discrepancies, the spiritual-formation practices must be adjusted to align with the given characteristics. The presence or lack of a specific characteristic in a disciple's life can be a valuable tool to evaluate their spiritual formation for missions. By observing how this trait is manifested in their life, one can gain insight into their missional readiness.

The idea of a faith community originated in the early Christian era. Christianity was the only known movement that brought together people from all walks of life, including men, women, children, and non-Jewish individuals, under one roof for worship. This unique aspect of Christianity made it all the more attractive, fascinating, and all-inclusive. In the same way, the communal aspect of a disciple's life is integral to their missional formation. Being part of a faith community that shares a common mission enables disciples to bear witness to non-believers as they engage in mission work together. Through this communal aspect, disciples can learn from others, be nurtured, and support each other. Being a part of a faith community that welcomes everyone, regardless of their background, exposes us to different cultures and helps us grow in the faith, serve others, and witness the transforming power of Christ.

How Can Christ's Disciples Be Communal?

Communal discipleship practices and expressions vary widely across Christian denominations and communities. Factors such as theological beliefs, cultural traditions, and historical contexts can influence these variations. For instance, some denominations may prioritize group Bible studies and prayer sessions as their primary discipleship practices, while others may emphasize mentoring relationships or service projects. Similarly, the expression of communal discipleship can be unique to the community, ranging from traditional liturgical practices to contemporary worship styles. Understanding these nuances can foster greater appreciation and respect for the diversity of Christian traditions.

Scriptural References for Communal Living

While no specific scripture is dedicated to communal living, several Bible passages highlight the importance of community, sharing, and mutual support among believers. Here are a few examples to help us grasp the vitality of communal living.

1. **Acts 2:42–47:** As we reflect on our actions, let us find ways to inspire and motivate one another toward acts of kindness and righteousness. We must not give up on our gatherings, as some may be prone to do, but instead, let us offer each other encouragement and support. Let us mainly focus on doing so as we approach the day, ensuring we are prepared for what lies ahead. This passage describes the early Christian community, where believers were devoted to teaching, fellowship, breaking bread, and prayer. They shared their possessions and took care of one another's needs.

2. **Romans 12:4–5:** "For just as each of us has one body with many members, and these members do not all have the same function, so in Christ we, though many, form one body, and each member belongs to all the others" (Rom 12:4–5). This Scripture is a symbolic representation of how the Body of Christ, composed of all believers, works together as a unified

entity. The comparison between the physical body and the Body of Christ highlights each member's different functions and emphasizes unity and cooperation. This means believers have distinct roles but are all equally important in the body's functioning. This is why the Church is composed of people from different backgrounds and walks of life who are united by their faith in Christ.

Moreover, Scripture suggests that believers should use their gifts and abilities to serve one another and maintain mutual respect and support. This means that each member of the Body of Christ should be mindful of their own needs and those of others in the body. This passage also highlights the importance of unity, collaboration, and mutual service among believers. As members of the same body, believers should recognize and celebrate their differences, work together for the greater good, and glorify God.

1. **Galatians 6:2:** "Carry each other's burdens, and in this way, you will fulfill the law of Christ." This speaks to the importance of offering support and assistance to our fellow believers. It reminds us that we are not meant to live in isolation but rather in community with one another. By carrying each other's burdens, we demonstrate our love and compassion toward our brothers and sisters in Christ. This verse is a call to action for believers to seek opportunities to help those struggling. It is a reminder that we are all in this together and are responsible for supporting and encouraging one another. Fulfilling the law of Christ is not just about following a set of rules but about living out our faith in a way that pleases God first and then benefits others. When we carry each other's

burdens, we fulfill our greatest commandment: to love our neighbors as ourselves. Let us take this passage to heart and seek ways to carry each other's burdens. I pray that our community will uphold the principles in these scriptures and provide love and support to those in need.

2. **Hebrews 10:24–25:** As followers of our faith, we are called to extend kindness toward one another and lend a helping hand in performing good deeds. We should not disregard church meetings, as some have been doing. Instead, we should regularly come together as a community to support and motivate one another. The need to gather and engage with one another now is more important than ever as the day of reckoning draws closer. This passage highlights the significance of congregating with fellow believers, as it fosters a sense of encouragement and inspiration toward love and good deeds.

3. **1 Corinthians 12:12–27:** This passage is a beautiful metaphor that likens the Church to the human body, comprised of many parts yet functioning as a single entity. Just as the human body has many parts, such as hands, feet, eyes, and ears, each with its unique function, the Body of Christ comprises individuals with specific gifts and abilities. The passage emphasizes the importance of each church member, regardless of their background or social status. It points out that every member is essential to the overall functioning of the Church, just as every part of the body is essential to its overall health and well-being. No part of the body is more important than the others, and the same is true of the Church.

Here, Apostle Paul emphasizes the need for church members to support and care for one another, just as the different parts of the body work together to keep the whole organism functioning correctly. When one member of the Church is in need, the other members must come together and offer support, just as the different parts of the body come together to support an injured limb. By valuing and supporting one another, we can create a strong and healthy community united by our shared faith in Christ. These are just a few examples. Many other verses emphasize the importance of community, sharing, and supporting one another as disciples of Christ. The Bible provides guidance and principles that can inform the practice of communal living for believers.

How Were the Disciples in the Bible Communal?

The disciples in the Bible exhibited communal aspects in various ways, as explained below.

Shared Mission and Purpose

A shared mission and purpose bound Jesus's disciples together. This mission was to live according to Jesus's teachings, learn from Him, and share His message with others. They were diverse individuals from different backgrounds, but their mutual devotion to Jesus united them. As they traveled with Jesus, they witnessed miracles, heard His teachings, and gained a deeper understanding of God's love and mercy. This experience strengthened their faith, and they became more confident in their role as Christ's followers.

In their journey together, they supported one another through difficult times and rejoiced in each other's successes. They formed a tight-knit community where they shared meals, stories, and prayers. This close bond made them more effective in spreading the message of Jesus, as they worked together in harmony. Their mission was not without challenges, as they faced persecution and rejection from some who did not believe in Jesus's message. However, their unwavering faith and commitment to their shared mission gave them the strength to persevere. Their communal living was marked by deepening their faith, strengthening their community, and committing to their shared mission and purpose.

Learning and Fellowship

The scene of the disciples gathering around Jesus is significant and rich in detail. Their goal was to learn from His teachings as they came together, but this gathering was much more than a classroom setting. The atmosphere was of fellowship and companionship, with the disciples spending time together, asking questions, and engaging in discussions. Meals were shared, which not only provided sustenance but also offered an opportunity for them to bond and grow closer together. This sense of community and camaraderie was essential to the disciples' growth as they learned from their teacher and one another. Through their shared experiences, the disciples developed a more profound understanding of their faith, creating a solid foundation for their future work.

Shared Resources

According to the gospels, Christ's disciples practiced communal living by sharing resources and pooling their belongings. This practice is evidenced in the book of Acts, "All the believers were one in heart and mind. No one claimed that any of their possessions was their own, but they shared everything they had" (Acts 4:32). This communal sharing was more than just a way of life for the disciples; it was an expression of their deep commitment to one another and Christ's teachings. It ensured that they met everyone's needs within the community and that no one was lacking. The disciples saw themselves as a family bound by their common faith and a shared sense of purpose. This way of living had its challenges, of course. It required a high level of trust and a willingness to put the needs of others before their own. However, the disciples believed this was true discipleship and were willing to make the sacrifices necessary to live this way.

Commissioned as a Group

In the gospels of Matthew and Luke, we read about Jesus commissioning His disciples for a specific task. He sent them out in pairs to minister to people, share the Good News, and proclaim God's kingdom. This was an essential moment in the history of Christianity, as it marked the beginning of the disciples' mission to spread the message of Jesus Christ to the world. Christ's choice to send out His disciples in pairs allowed them to work together, support each other, and share the responsibilities of their mission. The disciples were able to encourage one another during times of difficulty and celebrate the fruits of their labor together.

The commissioning of the disciples was not just a one-time event. It began a lifelong commitment to serving God and spreading the good news. The disciples followed Jesus's example and continued to minister to people, heal the sick, and share the message of salvation with those who needed it. This communal approach to ministry allowed them to support and encourage one another in their shared mission. Today, we can follow their example by working together, supporting one another, and sharing the message of hope and salvation with those around us.

Continued Fellowship After Jesus's Ascension

After Jesus ascended, His disciples did not scatter. Instead, they stayed together and formed a close-knit community. Acts 2:42–47 provides a meticulous account of the activities of these early believers. They were devoted to Jesus's teachings, always eager to learn more about Him and His message. They gathered regularly for fellowship, meals, and prayer. Their fellowship was not just a social activity but was rooted in their strong faith and common purpose. They supported one another through the ups and downs of life, offering a helping hand and a listening ear whenever needed. They shared their possessions and resources as required, ensuring no one was in need. The breaking of bread was a significant aspect of their fellowship. It was not just a simple act of sharing a meal but a commemorative event, reminding them of Jesus's sacrifice on the cross. This ritual strengthened their bond and renewed their commitment to follow in their Lord's footsteps.

The disciples' relationships emphasize the significance of community and mutual support in their pursuit of following Jesus and sharing His message. Their experiences demonstrate that discipleship involves a shared responsibility and commitment to the greater mission. The disciples overcame challenges and persevered in their journey by relying on one another's strengths and resources. This highlights the importance of collaboration and connection to achieve common goals. Ultimately, their communal nature and shared purpose served as a driving force for their success. After Christ's ascension, the disciples formed a vibrant, dynamic community characterized by devotion to His teachings, fellowship, sharing possessions, breaking bread, and prayer. Their actions testified to their deep faith and commitment to the gospel.

How Can We Practice Communal Living?

As Christians, there are several practical ways to foster a sense of community and live communally with people from various walks of life. Here are some valuable suggestions.

Regular Fellowship

If you want to deepen your walk with Christ and form strong bonds with other believers, joining a Christian community that practices communal living may be an excellent option. Communal living provides a unique opportunity to share your life with others who share your faith and experience a more profound sense of community that can be difficult to find today. Participate regularly with other believers to get the most out of this communal experience. Attending worship services, joining small groups, and engaging in Bible studies are great ways to connect with others and grow in your faith. These gatherings provide a safe, welcoming space to share feelings and thoughts, ask questions, and learn from others.

By engaging in regular fellowship with other believers, you can build full-bodied relationships that can last a lifetime. You will also be able to support and encourage one another through good and bad times and grow together in your faith as you explore God's Word and apply it to your lives. If you seek a way to strengthen your faith and connect with others, consider joining a Christian community that practices communal living. Regular fellowship and engagement will give you the love, support, and encouragement to thrive in your walk with Christ.

Acts of Service

We are called to serve others and make a difference in our communities. One way to do this is by seeking opportunities to volunteer, using our time and talents to support those in need. This can be done through local outreach programs, charity initiatives, or faithfully serving in your church. Serving others not only helps to meet their practical needs but also cultivates a sense of communal care and selflessness within us. When we put the needs of others before our own, we reflect the heart of Jesus and demonstrate His love to the world. By serving others, we can substantially affect the lives of those we encounter. Whether volunteering at a homeless shelter, participating in a community clean-up, or simply lending a helping hand to someone in need, we can bring hope and joy to others. Let us strive to be servants of Christ, always looking for ways to bless those around us.

Sharing Resources

Sharing resources in this context means giving away something we possess to someone who needs it. This could include material possessions, financial assistance, or practical help. By sharing our resources with others, we foster a sense of communal support and solidarity. Sharing material possessions might mean lending a book, giving away clothes that no longer fit, or sharing your car for a carpool. Offering financial assistance could mean giving money to a friend going through a tough time or donating to a charity. Providing practical help could mean offering to babysit for a neighbor who needs to run errands or helping a friend move into a new apartment. When we share our resources, we are not only helping others; we are also building stronger connections within our communities. We show that we care and are willing to lend a helping hand when needed. So, let's try to be more generous and willing to share what we have with those around us.

Prayer and Encouragement

As believers, we are called to offer prayers and encouragement to one another to build a solid and supportive community. This involves listening, supporting, and uplifting our fellow believers through heartfelt words of affirmation and prayer. By taking the time to empathize with the struggles and joys of our community, we create an environment of love and support that fosters spiritual growth and healing. When we offer prayers for one another, we lift each other to God and strengthen our bonds of fellowship. Encouraging one another through kind words and expressions of empathy can profoundly impact our spiritual and holistic well-being, helping us feel valued and supported in our walk of faith. So, I encourage you to make a conscious effort to prioritize prayer and encouragement within your community. Doing so can create a culture of compassion and support that reflects God's love and grace.

Hospitality

Hospitality is not merely serving in the hospitality department of your church alone. It is the act of opening up your home or arms and extending a warm welcome to others. It involves creating a comfortable and inviting atmosphere to gather, share meals, and enjoy one another's company. When you extend hospitality, you invite people into your life, fostering deeper connections and relationships among community members. Inviting fellow believers for meals, gatherings, or times of fellowship is a great way to practice hospitality. Sharing a meal with someone goes beyond the act of eating. It is a moment of connection where you get to share your thoughts, stories, and feelings while nourishing your body and soul. It is a time to bond with others, create memories, and strengthen relationships. It is also a time to share stories, experiences, and laughter and to build bonds of trust and friendship. Understand that hospitality is not just about the food you serve or the environment you create. It is also about the warmth and love you extend to your guests. When you welcome others into your home, you show them they are valued and essential. You are creating a space where they can feel comfortable and safe and be themselves without fear of judgment. In a world that can be cold and impersonal, hospitality is a way to bring warmth and humanity back into our lives. So, let us all practice hospitality and create welcoming spaces where everyone feels valued and loved.

Accountability and Mentorship

Developing a robust support system is crucial to maintaining a healthy spiritual life. One of the best ways to do this is by seeking accountability and mentorship within your community. Find trustworthy individuals who share similar values and beliefs and who can provide guidance and support and hold you accountable when needed. Accountability partners can help you remain on track and furnish you with structure and discipline as you carry your cross daily. They can also provide a listening ear and contribute productive feedback when necessary. Similarly, having a mentor can be an invaluable resource for those striving to elevate their spiritual understanding and practice.

A mentor can guide you through their experiences and wisdom and help you navigate the challenges that arise. Of course, accountability and mentorship are not one-way streets. It is also crucial to offer yourself as a mentor or accountability partner to others. By sharing your experiences and offering your support, you can help others grow in their faith and deepen their relationship with God. Spiritual maturation is a voyage that demands commitment, discipline, and support. You can ensure you are never alone on this journey by cultivating a community of accountability and mentorship.

Communal Living Is a Journey

Living in a Christian community requires effort and dedication. It is an ongoing process that involves building relationships, sharing experiences, and supporting one another in faith. To contribute to the community's growth and vibrancy, you can attend worship services, participate in Bible studies, volunteer for community service projects, and reach out to fellow members in need. These acts strengthen your faith in God. They also play crucial roles in building a supportive and uplifting environment for everyone in the community.

Why Are So Many Christian Disciples Lone Rangers?

Personal Choice

Discipleship is a personal journey, and some people prefer to embark on this journey alone. This decision may stem from various reasons, including the desire for a more individualistic approach to their relationship with God and the study of Scripture. These individuals may choose to live out their faith more independently, free from the influence of others, to develop a deeper understanding of their beliefs. Some believe that studying Scripture provides a more personalized experience that allows for a more profound connection with the divine.

Lack of Community

There are times when individuals seek access to a supportive Christian community or participate in one but may face various challenges when connecting with like-minded believers who share similar values and beliefs. These difficulties may arise due to a need for more awareness of resources or proximity to a faith-based community. Moreover, certain individuals may have specific needs or situations that require specialized support, such as counseling or mentorship programs. Additionally, some individuals may have experienced alienation or rejection from past church communities, making them apprehensive about engaging with new ones. As a result, they may have difficulty finding a church or fellowship group that provides a sense of belonging and support.

This lack of a supportive Christian community can lead to feelings of isolation, disconnection, and even spiritual emptiness. Therefore, we must address these concerns and provide resources that cater to the diverse needs of individuals seeking to be part of a supportive Christian community. This can be done through outreach programs, counseling services, mentorship programs, and support groups that cater to specific needs. By providing these resources, individuals can find a community that offers the support and encouragement they need to grow in their faith and live fulfilling lives.

Cultural Influences

The cultural environment within which a person resides plays a critical role in shaping their understanding and practice of discipleship. I cannot overemphasize the impact of cultural influences on an individual's perception of faith. In some cultures, there is a strong emphasis on individualism, which places more value on self-reliance and independence. This, in turn, may lead to a more personalized and self-directed approach to a community of faith. In such cultural contexts, the concept of community of faith may not be as prevalent as in other societies where communal engagement in faith is more highly valued.

Additionally, some Christians may feel that their personal beliefs or practices differ from those of their local faith community, which can lead them to seek alternative ways of expressing their faith. Therefore, we must consider a person's cultural background when understanding their discipleship approach. We should also acknowledge that different cultural contexts significantly affect how individuals approach their spiritual journey. When reaching out to this group, we should be careful never to water down the gospel to reach them. The idea is to bring them to God and not reduce God to attract them.

Bitter Experiences

When individuals experience adverse incidents or conflicts within Christian communities, it can have a continuing effect on their spiritual pilgrimage. These experiences may manifest as feelings of pain, disappointment, or disillusionment, which can then lead individuals to choose a more solitary path. By avoiding communal discipleship, they may feel they are protecting themselves from further negative interactions. As a result, these individuals may prioritize their personal spiritual growth and development. They may have to study the Bible, pray, and practice meditation to deepen their relationship with God. While they may still attend church services or participate in community events, they may do so with a sense of caution or hesitation. Ultimately, their past experiences shape their approach to faith and influence their decision to pursue a more solitary path.

Sense of Fulfillment and Purpose

Christ's life and teachings emphasize the importance of community, fellowship, and mutual support in great detail, despite some individuals choosing to be more self-reliant in their discipleship. In establishing a community of disciples, Jesus emphasized the significance of learning from and supporting one another and the importance of building relationships with fellow believers. The New Testament consistently stresses the necessity of believers coming together and serving one another spiritually and practically.

For those who may feel like a "lone ranger" in their faith journey, seeking out opportunities for community and connection with fellow believers can be transformative. Engaging in a supportive

Christian community can offer accountability, growth, and the chance to share in the faith journey's joys and challenges in much greater detail. Doing so can strengthen our faith and help others do the same by building more profound and meaningful relationships of mutual support and encouragement. Moreover, a supportive Christian community provides a sense of belonging and purpose and helps us live out our faith practically. For instance, by serving and helping others in the community, we can put our faith into action and make a tangible difference in the lives of those around us. The sense of fulfillment and purpose that comes from serving others and being a part of a community can be transformative, deepening our faith and commitment to living a Christ-centered life.

For Reflection

1. In what ways do you participate in your faith community? Are you attending religious services, participating in community events, or engaging in spiritual practices with others? What actions can you take to deepen your involvement and enrich your experience within your faith community?

2. How can you strengthen and enrich your relationships with the people around you? When conflicts or disagreements arise within your community, what strategies do you employ to resolve them?

3. How do you ensure that you are living up to the ethical standards and beliefs of the faith community to which you belong?

4. How do you hold yourself accountable and ensure you contribute positively to your faith community apart from tithes and offerings?

Food For Thought

Discipleship is not just a mere belief, religion, or a ticket to heaven but a way of life that transforms your heart, mind, and actions. It is a call to love and serve others in humility, as that is how we live a life that reflects Christ's character.

Ten

A DISCIPLE IS A HUMBLE SERVANT

> *Whosoever will be chief among you, let the person first be your*
> *servant: even as the Son of man came . . . to minister." "They*
> *that humbles themselves shall be exalted.*
>
> **Matthew 10:27–28, Luke 18:14**

Humility is a quality that often eludes many people, yet it is essential for personal growth and well-being. One of the critical aspects of humility is the ability to recognize and accept your limitations. When we are honest with ourselves, we can treat others with kindness and respect. The question arises: "Can you identify the signs that indicate that you possess humility?" It is easy to think of ourselves as humble before God, but that alone does not prove our humility. Your humility before your fellow human beings is a genuine measure of your humility before God. It requires an empathetic and compassionate approach, putting ourselves in other people's shoes and treating them with dignity and respect. When we practice humility, it takes root within us and positively shapes our lives. We become more open-minded, tolerant, and accepting of others and better equipped to handle life's challenges. Luke 9:14–17 teaches us that a true disciple is a humble servant.

Jesus's disciples were not afraid to get their hands dirty. They worked tirelessly to distribute the multiplied food to the people—their selflessness and willingness to help others demonstrate the true spirit of humility. Sometimes, walking with Jesus means humbling yourself to serve others. Humility and servanthood go together. While on earth, Jesus demonstrated His heart for people. He served His disciples while leading them to practice servanthood. Humble servants are never motivated by what they will gain in the end. They are motivated by serving people. The Apostle Paul also dealt seriously with this issue when he urged the people of Philippians to imitate Christ's humility. He introduced himself to the church in Rome first as a servant, then as an apostle. In his letter, he wrote, "Paul, a servant of Christ Jesus, called to be an apostle and set apart for the Gospel of God" (Rom. 1:1). Apostle Paul stresses the implications of humility in our day-to-day interaction. He advises us to honor and prefer one another, to avoid egotism, and to condescend to people of low estate.

In Corinthians, Paul underscores that love cannot exist without humility, as it is not puffed up, does not vaunt itself, and is not easily provoked. In Galatians, he teaches us to serve one another with love, not to be desirous of vain glory, and not to provoke or envy one another. In Ephesians, Paul advises us to walk with all lowliness, meekness, and suffering in love and to subject ourselves to one another in fear of God. In Philippians, he encourages us to esteem others as better than ourselves, to have the mind of Christ who humbled Himself, and to let nothing be done through faction or vainglory. Finally, in Colossians, Paul tells us to be merciful, kind, humble, meek, and long-suffering, to forbear and forgive one another, even as Christ forgave us.

One of the characteristics that a disciple should be known for is their dedication to Christ. Throughout His time on Earth, Christ exemplified the highest level of humility, especially in the way He made His heart vulnerable to us. His sacrificial life makes it so challenging to be a true disciple of Christ without strict adherence to His teaching. The thing about Christ is that He speaks of it and expects His followers, especially those who claim to be His disciples, to be as humble as He was. I encourage you to study the passages that portray His sacrificial life so you can grasp the full extent of how often and how earnestly Christ taught humility. It will help you fathom what Christ asks of His disciples. Let's look at how Christ's ministry commenced through His teachings on the Mount of Olives, commonly known as the Beatitudes.

As recorded in Matthew 5:3, 5, Jesus said, "Blessed are the poor in spirit, for theirs is the kingdom of heaven. Blessed are the meek, for they shall inherit the earth." These utterances reveal His public declaration of the kingdom of heaven and the only gate through which we can all enter it. His declaration reveals that earthly and heavenly blessings are for the lowly. This insinuates that humility is the secret of blessing in both the earthly and the divine life. As Jesus says in Matthew 11:29, "Learn of me; for I am meek and lowly of heart: and ye shall find rest unto your souls." Again, Jesus is pouring Himself out to teach us and to help us understand what it means to be a humble servant. As He projected in the Sermon on the Mount and this passage, lowliness and meekness are the significant things Christ offers His disciples. In this sacrificial offering, we find the perfect rest of the soul, which portrays humility as a salvific path to the kingdom of heaven.

Luke 9:46 and Matthew 18:3 recount a memorable day when the disciples got into a heated argument about who among them would be the greatest in God's kingdom. After much debate, they turned to their master, Jesus Christ, for guidance. With a calm demeanor, Jesus placed a young child in their midst and said, "Anyone who becomes as humble as this little child is the greatest in the kingdom of heaven" (Mt 18:4–5). Through this profound statement, Jesus revealed that true excellence is measured by humility. Additionally, Jesus stated that whoever is the least among them is the greatest. The disciples were perplexed and continued to ask Jesus questions about their status in the kingdom. When the sons of Zebedee asked to sit on Christ's right and left, the highest places in the kingdom, He explained that only the Father can reward those who humble themselves as servants first. This tells us that humility in service is the measure of true greatness in God's kingdom.

Therefore, Christians should approach their desires and requests with a sense of humility and a willingness to serve others. This reminds Christians to keep the cross and the humility that comes with it at the forefront of their thoughts. Being a true disciple demands that we serve others and strive to do so humbly. Christ exemplified this by putting others before Himself and ultimately giving His life for the salvation of many. Therefore, to become a great leader, we must have the heart of a servant.

Humility is a defining characteristic of Christ in heaven and will be the standard of glory in the afterlife. The most humble Christian among us will be the closest to God. In the Church, those who display humility should be granted the highest positions of authority. In a discussion about God's kingdom, Jesus addressed His disciples, the crowds, and even the Pharisees, saying, "The greatest among you must be a servant" (Mt 23:11). This serves as a reminder that true greatness comes not from power, money, or status but from our willingness to serve others with humility. It is also the only stepladder to honor in the kingdom of heaven. This aligns with what Jesus says in Matthew 23:12, "But those who exalt themselves

will be humbled, and those who humble themselves will be exalted."
In teaching about self-abasement in the Pharisee's house, Jesus saw
an opportunity that led Him to address the pressing matter of
humility in Luke 14:1–11. He addressed the issue when He noticed
how the guests picked the places of honor at the table.

When you are invited to a ceremony, Christ said, wait to take
the place of honor until the host does so. Why? To save you from
unnecessary public humiliation. This is because you don't know if a
person more distinguished than you will show up or a more distinguished fellow might have been invited. If so, the host who invited
both of you will come and tell you to give this person your seat.
Then, humiliated publicly, you must take the least important place
in shame. Christ warns that when you are invited, first of all, take
the lowest place so that when your host comes, he will say to you,
"Sir/ma'am, move up to a more honorable place." This is how you
get honored in the presence of all the other guests. In other words,
Jesus advises us not to make ourselves the guest of honor and to
allow the host to elevate us to a more honorable seat. He ends his
speech by saying, "For all those who exalt themselves, you will be
humbled, and to those who humble themselves, they will always be
exalted."[1]

Just so you can comprehend how critical the issue of service
and humility is to Jesus, after the parable of the Pharisee and the
Publican, He warns again, "For all those who exalt themselves will
be humbled, and those who humble themselves will be exalted" (Lk
18:14). In the temple and the presence and worship of God, everything is worthless that is not pervaded by deep, genuine humility
and selfless service toward God and others. Reflecting on washing His disciples' feet, Jesus instructed His disciples to serve with
humility: "Now that I, your Lord and Teacher, have washed your
feet, it is imperative that you also wash one another's feet. I have
set an example that you, my disciples, should do as I have done for

you." He further asserts that no servant is more significant than his master, nor are any of us greater than Christ. This is one of those instructions for a disciple that comes with a blessing.

You can no longer claim you don't know, especially after reading this book. Now that we can all agree that you have learned these things, you will be incredibly blessed if you do them according to what you have seen Christ do or read about Him (Jn 13:14–17). This also conforms with James's teaching in James 1:22–25, "Do not merely listen to the word, and so deceive yourselves. Do what it says. . . But whoever looks intently into the very Word of God that gives freedom and continues in it, not forgetting what they have heard but doing it, will be blessed beyond bounds in what they do."[2] Speaking of James, if you study the first verse of James, you will see an utmost display of servanthood and humility. Even though James was a stepbrother to Jesus, James addresses himself as a servant of God and the Lord Jesus Christ. His humility as a disciple of Jesus is noteworthy. The authority of Christ's instructions, example, teachings, and obedience make service and humility the most essential element of discipleship, as it takes a selfless heart and humility to harken to the call for discipleship.

Through lifelong spiritual formation, disciples become faithful servants of Christ. If you are a disciple and people are still grappling with or questioning your servanthood, it means you are exhibiting a sense of pride. Pride should not be present in a disciple's life. Andrew Murray argues that "the root and essence of all Jesus's character as our redeemer is nothing but His humility."[3] The heart filled with the humility of Christ is the only medium in which Jesus lives and grows. Jesus also taught people about washing feet, which symbolized serving others. It's not enough to be humble before God if we don't also show humility toward others. We must respect and be kind to others, regardless of their background, race, or status. The essence of humility lies in a willingness to serve others and to honor them above ourselves. It is a way of life that involves esteeming others as better than ourselves, submitting to one another, and being the servant of all. However, adopting this way of life is difficult, especially when others seem far below us regarding wisdom, holiness, natural gifts, or grace received. In this passage, let us look deeper at this well-crafted message of humility and service.

Therefore, if you have any encouragement from being united with Christ, if any comfort from his love, if any common sharing in the spirit, if any tenderness and compassion, then make my joy complete by being like-minded, having the same love, being one in spirit and of one mind. Do nothing out of selfish ambition or vain conceit. Rather, in humility, value others above yourselves, not looking to your interests but each of you to the interests of the others. In your relationships with one another, have the same mindset as Christ Jesus: Who, being in very nature[a] God, did not consider equality with God something to be used to his advantage; rather, he made himself nothing by taking the very nature of a servant, being made in human likeness. And being found in appearance as a man, he humbled himself by becoming obedient to death, even death on a cross! Therefore, God exalted him to the highest place and gave him the name above every name, that in the name of Jesus, every knee should bow in heaven, on earth, and under the earth. Every tongue acknowledges that Jesus Christ is Lord, to the glory of God the Father. (Phil 2:1–11)

This passage drives home the message of humility and service. It tells us that there is no true discipleship without a heart of humble service. Christ poured out His life for us through His endless sacrifice, humility, and obedience, even unto death on the cross. For this reason, God exalted His Son to the highest place and gave Him the name above every name. True disciples must emulate His example of humility and carry out Christ's teachings on humility and servanthood. Humility should be a disciple's top priority. Murray also urges us to listen to the words in which our Lord speaks of His relation to the Father and how unceasingly he uses the words "not" and "nothing" of Himself (Jn 5:19, 5:30, 5:41, 7:16, 8:50).[4] Also, John 13:1–17 describes Jesus's performance of this act of humility. In verses 13:14–17, Christ instructs His disciples, saying, "If I, Jesus, your Lord, and your Teacher could bend down and wash your feet, you should also wash one another's feet as a mark of humility. As you can see, I just gave you an example, so serve others as I have served you." This account shows humility and servanthood as the first and the all-inclusive grace of Christ's life. Acts 1:8 is a paradigmatic verse for the program of Acts and the servant role of disciples.[5] This verse features the call of the servant role. After Jesus promised them the Holy Spirit, He stated that they would be His witnesses in Jerusalem, in all Judea and Samaria, and to the ends of the earth (Acts 1:8). The Great Commission cannot be achieved without humble servants.

How to Practice Humility and Servanthood

Practicing humility and servanthood involves embodying the character and teachings of Jesus Christ. In God's presence, we meet our fellow human beings as equals, not superiors or inferiors. We try to serve them, honor them, and love them as God's children. Even if we are wiser than our masters, we still adopt the spirit and posture of a servant, just like Jesus washed the disciples' feet. By following Jesus's example, a humble disciple brings glory to God and reflects the transformative power of Christ's love in the world.

Esteem Others

Humble disciples value and esteem others. They recognize the worth and dignity of every individual, treating them with respect, kindness, and compassion. They listen attentively, empathize with others' struggles, and seek to meet people where they are. Being a humble servant means imitating Jesus in attitude and action. It involves cultivating a humble heart, serving others selflessly, and demonstrating sacrificial love. To practice humility, we must let go of our ego and make God the center of our lives. When we see ourselves as insignificant before God, we can appreciate the essence of humility. When we lose ourselves in finding God, we stop comparing ourselves with others and seeking anything for ourselves.

Serve Others

A humble disciple has a heart for serving others. They enjoy putting the needs of others before their own. They look for opportunities to serve, whether in small acts of kindness or more prominent acts of sacrificial love. They serve with a genuine desire to bless and uplift others without seeking recognition or personal gain. I encourage you to be on the lookout for opportunities to serve those around you. This could involve acts of kindness, helping those in need, volunteering in your community, or serving in your local church. Please be aware of others ' needs and offer your time, resources, and abilities to meet those needs.

Practice Active Listening

Cultivate the habit of genuinely listening to others. When conversing, please give them your full attention, seek to understand their perspective, and empathize with their joys and struggles. Engage in conversations with genuine interest and humility, making others feel valued and heard.

Put Others First

Christlike humility involves recognizing our position before God and others and acknowledging that we depend on God's grace and mercy. It means having a modest view of yourself without pride or arrogance. A humble disciple understands that their worth comes from being a child of God and seeks to imitate the humility of Jesus. The humble person values every weak and seemingly unworthy child of God, recognizing that they, too, are created in God's image and deserve our respect and love. They honor others and prefer them as if they were the children of a king, knowing that we are all equal in God's eyes.

A humble servant does not seek positions of prominence or recognition. Instead, they willingly take the lowest place, preferring to serve from a position of humility and allowing others to be lifted. They do not vie for power or status but seek to serve as Jesus did, with humility and selflessness. Prioritize the needs and interests of others above your own. Instead of seeking personal recognition or advancement, look for ways to support and uplift others. Be willing to take a backseat and let others shine. Celebrate the successes and accomplishments of those around you without jealousy or comparison.

Cultivate a Teachable Spirit

We all have much to learn. This means being open to receiving instruction and correction from others. Instead of thinking you know it all, acknowledge your limitations, mistakes, and areas that require growth. One of the best ways to learn and grow is to seek wisdom from others. This can come in many forms, such as mentors, trusted friends, and the guidance of the Holy Spirit.

Mentors can provide valuable insight and advice based on their experiences and expertise. Trusted friends can offer a different perspective and support when needed. And seeking the guidance of the Holy Spirit can provide clarity and direction in your life. Embrace a lifelong posture of learning and growth. This means seeking new knowledge and skills and being willing to adapt and change as circumstances and situations demand. By remaining open to learning and development, you can become the best possible version of yourself and achieve your goals and dreams.

Seek Opportunities to Serve Behind the Scenes

Adopt a service mindset. Take on tasks and responsibilities that benefit others, even if they are menial or go unnoticed. Disciples are willing to serve in various capacities, using their gifts, time, and resources to meet the needs of others. Look for ways to serve without seeking recognition or praise. Serve in areas where your contributions may go unnoticed but are necessary for the smooth functioning of a ministry or organization. This could involve tasks such as cleaning, organizing, or administrative work.

Develop a Heart of Gratitude

Cultivate an attitude of gratitude for all that God has blessed you with. Recognize that everything you have is a gift from Him, and express appreciation to others for their contributions and kindness. Avoid feelings of entitlement or a sense of superiority. Instead, approach life with humility and thankfulness.

Pray for Humility

Ask God to cultivate humility in your heart. Recognize your dependence on Him, and invite Him to shape your character. Pray for the strength to resist pride, arrogance, and self-centeredness and embrace Christ's servant-hearted nature. Humility and servanthood are lifelong endeavors. Each day, seek to live out these qualities in your interactions with others, relying on the Holy Spirit's guidance and transformation in your life. By practicing humility and servanthood, you reflect Christ's love and become a witness to His transformative power in the world.

Strive for a More Fulfilling Christian Life

When striving for a more fulfilling Christian life, it's easy to focus on what could be called human virtues, such as boldness, joy, contempt for the world, zeal, and self-sacrifice. These are virtues that even the Stoics taught and practiced. However, we shouldn't overlook the deeper and gentler graces connected with Jesus's teachings, such as poverty of the spirit, meekness, humility, and lowliness. Unfortunately, these graces are often undervalued and do not receive the attention they deserve.

Do Not Be Discouraged by the Church's Lack of Humility

Humble people don't feel envious. Even when others are preferred and blessed, they praise God for the good in others. They don't mind being overlooked or forgotten because they know they are significant in God's presence. The humble spirit follows the example of Jesus, who didn't seek to please Himself or promote His honor. When dealing with fellow Christians who may stumble and sin, the humble person is wise to remember this warning: if someone has done wrong to you, be patient and forgiving. Colossians 3:13 encourages us to follow the Lord's example. By putting on the Lord Jesus Christ, we are also called to put on a heart filled with compassion, kindness, humility, meekness, and patience. This transformation helps us become more humble and understanding toward others.

I understand that the Church may be suffering from a lack of humility. This lack of humility prevents God from being able to demonstrate His power. Recently, I had a conversation with a brother who expressed deep sorrow over the way some mission stations portrayed a lack of the spirit of love and forbearance. He explained how difficult it can be for men and women to come together in unity of the gospel and how hard it is for them to bear, love, and keep the unity of the spirit in the bond of peace. They allow their pride to get in the way of spiritual matters. The root cause of this problem is the lack of humility. If not, why is it hard for people who have given themselves up for Christ to give themselves up for their brothers and sisters in Christ? The Church has not taught its children that the humility of Christ is the first virtue, the best of all the graces and powers of the Spirit. They have not shown that Christlike humility is genuinely needed and possible. Let us not be discouraged by the lack of this grace in the Church. Instead, let us allow it to stir more considerable expectations from God.

We should look upon everyone who tries or vexes us as God's means of grace and as an instrument for our purification. We should exercise the humility that Jesus breathes within us. We should have such faith in God that we seek only to serve one another in love, considering ourselves nothing in our own eyes. True humility is not something we put on temporarily during prayer but an integral part of our daily behavior. How we act in small, everyday situations shows our true character. We can learn a lot about someone's nature by observing their behavior in daily life. As you watch others, they are also watching you, so be humble and make it a habit.

Notes

[1] Luke 14:1–11, Jesus at a Pharisee's House.

[2] James 1:22–25, paraphrased.

[3] Andrew Murray, *Humility* (Nashville, TN: B&H Publishing Group, 2017), 24, https://app.wordsearchbible.lifeway.com.

[4] Ibid, 26.

[5] Holly Beers, "'Acts and the Servant.' The Followers of Jesus as the 'Servant,'" *Luke's Model from Isaiah for the Disciples in Luke–Acts* (2015): 126–175.

Self-Reflection Time

1. How do you define humility? In what ways do you practice humility in your daily life?

2. Discipleship is not just a mere belief but a way of life that transforms your heart, mind, and actions. Reflect on this statement and then discuss how it resonates with your thoughts on discipleship.

3. Have you ever struggled with pride or self-centeredness? If so, how can you cultivate a more humble and servant-hearted attitude?

4. Share some of the challenges you have faced while serving others. How did you overcome them? How can you continue to develop as a humble servant?

5. What steps can you take to enhance your ability to serve others with greater effectiveness and humility?

Food For Thought

Faith does not excuse competence and integrity. Know how to do your job, and do it to the best of your ability, as only your best is ever good enough.

Eleven

A DISCIPLE IS A GOOD STEWARD

> *Remember that each of us possesses unique abilities and resources God has bestowed upon us. We must use these abilities and resources to help one another and spread the abundance of blessings that God has bestowed upon us.*
>
> **1 Peter 4:10**

Responsible stewardship is crucial to following Christ, and it involves recognizing our responsibility to manage the gifts and blessings God has bestowed upon us. We must always use our talents, time, and finances to promote justice, love, and compassion toward others. Ultimately, being a responsible steward means recognizing that all of these resources are gifts from God and that we are called to use them in a manner that is consistent with His will. Doing so can honor God and bring blessings to those around us. One of the best examples of being a good steward is when we take care of the environment. We must be mindful of our impact on the planet and ensure we responsibly use its resources. This includes reducing waste, conserving energy, and using sustainable practices. By doing so, we can ensure that future generations can enjoy the same blessings and gifts we have been given. Here are a few critical aspects of being a good steward as a disciple:

Critical Aspects of Good Stewardship

Recognition of Ownership

Recognizing that everything we possess is ultimately God's property is crucial. We are not the owners but rather the caretakers or managers of the resources that God has entrusted to us. This viewpoint cultivates a sense of gratitude, humility, and accountability in handling those resources. It reminds us that we are responsible for the stewardship of the resources we have been given and must use them wisely and judiciously. This perspective also highlights the importance of treating our resources carefully and not merely as disposable commodities. Ultimately, acknowledging that we are not owners but caretakers of God's resources can lead to a deeper appreciation of their value and inspire us to use them to benefit ourselves, others, and the world around us.

Faithful Management

Managing our resources is a crucial aspect of our lives. Being diligent, wise, and faithful in managing these resources is essential to leading a meaningful and fulfilling life. We must be mindful of how we use our time, talents, and finances and ensure they align with God's purposes and values. This requires us to make intentional choices rooted in faith and honor God while contributing to His kingdom. By being faithful managers, we can positively impact society and actively participate in creating a better world for ourselves and future generations.

Generosity and Sharing

It is crucial to consistently display a spirit of generosity and sharing towards others, regardless of race, religion, or social status. We must recognize that the blessings we receive from God are not just for our enjoyment but also to bless others. Generosity requires us to be willing to help those in need and support God's work. Sharing can take many forms. It could mean sacrificing our time, talents, or resources to help someone in need. It could also mean sharing our material possessions, such as food, clothing, or shelter, with less fortunate people. It also requires us to look for opportunities to help others and be willing to go out of our way to do so.

Moreover, generosity and sharing have a ripple effect. Helping someone in need and inspiring them to do the same for others creates a positive chain reaction. Our efforts can impact the lives of others and contribute to building a better and more compassionate world. Our actions also help spread God's love and compassion to needy people.

Financial Stewardship

Financial stewardship is an essential aspect of managing our finances. It contains a broad spectrum of practices, such as creating a budget, saving money, avoiding excessive debt, and using our financial resources that align with biblical principles. By being responsible with our income, giving generously, and using our resources wisely, we can better meet our needs and fulfill our God-given responsibilities. Financial stewardship requires careful planning and discernment and a willingness to prioritize our finances to reflect our values and beliefs. Ultimately, it is about being good stewards of the resources God has entrusted to us and using them to create a more secure and fulfilling future for ourselves and those around us.

Time Management

Time management is an indispensable part of our day-to-day living that requires careful consideration and planning. It requires intentionally allocating time and prioritizing activities aligning with our values, beliefs, and faith. When managing our time, it is imperative to prioritize activities that contribute to our spiritual growth, relationships, and mission. One way to prioritize your time is by carving out dedicated and intentional time for prayer, studying the Scriptures, serving others, and building meaningful connections with those around us. These activities help us grow spiritually, foster our relationships with others, and enable us to serve God through our communities.

Successful finance and time management also involve being mindful of financial distractions and time-wasters that hinder us from achieving our goals. Money itself is good, but how we manage our longing for it and how we manage it when we control it impacts our lives. Godliness is the result of a biblically disciplined spiritual life. I believe that the core of a disciplined spiritual life is our attitude toward using time and managing the resources God has blessed us with, including money. For example, if you manage your time well, you will not have to overwork your engine only to race and exceed the speed limit to get to work. You will not have that speeding ticket if you do not exceed the speed limit. The ticket alone puts a hole in your finances, and that is the money you could use for something else. When this lifestyle continues, it creates myriads of problems for us, making it difficult to enjoy more blessings from God.

It also creates more waste that may gradually lead to suffering, poverty, or mental health issues. This may be because "One who is faithful in a very little is also faithful in much, and one who is dishonest in a very little is also dishonest in much (Luke 16:10).

Paying less attention to how we follow the clock or mismanaging the dollar can negatively impact us in such a way that may lead to anxiety, depression, anger, divorce, and the list goes on. Each of the anxiety or stress producers relates to either time or money in one way or the other. The clock and the dollar are such substantial factors in so many parts of life that we must consider their role in any serious discussion of godly living. Remember, 1 Timothy 6:10 warned that the intense desire for wealth and material possessions has been identified as the source of various forms of evil. As a consequence of pursuing this desire, many individuals have deviated from their moral values and caused themselves a great deal of distress and suffering.

Care for Creation

As followers of God, we are responsible for caring for His creation. We must be aware of the impact of our actions on the environment and take steps to be good stewards of the earth. This involves practicing sustainability, reducing waste, and supporting initiatives that promote environmental stewardship. Practicing sustainability means using resources to meet your needs without compromising the capability of forthcoming generations to satisfy their necessities. It involves making choices that minimize negative environmental consequences, such as utilizing renewable energy sources and lowering our carbon footprint.

Reducing waste is another important aspect of environmental stewardship. Consider reducing the amount of waste you produce by being mindful of what you consume and how you dispose of it. This may involve recycling, composting, or reducing our use of single-use plastics. Supporting initiatives that promote environmental stewardship is godly. This can include advocating for policies protecting the environment, supporting organizations that preserve natural habitats, or participating in community clean-up efforts. Living with a stewardship mindset can fulfill our duty to care for the earth. It can also positively impact future generations.

Practical Ways of Being A Good Steward

Make it your goal to live a peaceful or quiet life by minding your business and working with your hands, just as we instructed you. By doing so, you will earn the respect of those who may not share your beliefs and gain the independence you need to flourish.

1 Thessalonians 4:11-12 (Paraphrased)

Being a good steward involves a holistic approach to managing your life grounded in biblical principles of responsibility and faithfulness. These areas may include your finances, relationships, time, talents, and resources. 1 Thessalonians 4:11-12 urges us to strive for a quiet life by minding our own business and working diligently with whatever our hands find to do. This quiet life will earn the respect of those who may not share your views or beliefs while you gain the independence you require to develop and grow to your fullest potential. You will also not only honor God but also experience the blessings of a life well-lived.

To be a good steward, you must intentionally manage your finances wisely, live within your means, and avoid debt. Building and maintaining healthy relationships, investing time in personal growth, and using your talents to serve others are paramount to being a good steward. Additionally, good stewards take good care of the resources they have been given, such as their home, transportation, and possessions. It also involves good stewardship habits like maintenance, repair, and reuse. Here are some practical ways to be a good steward as a disciple:

Time & Money

As the book of Wisdom teaches, "There is a time for everything, and a season for every activity under the heavens..." (Ecclesiastes 3:1-8, NIV). Prioritize your time and use it wisely. Set aside regular moments for prayer, reading and studying the Bible, and engaging in meaningful relationships. Avoid time-wasting activities that distract you from pursuing God's purposes. Create a budget and practice wise financial management. Give generously to support the church's work and help those in need. Avoid excessive debt and be mindful of your spending habits. Seek God's guidance in financial decisions and strive to be content with what you have.

Talents and Abilities

Identify and use your unique talents and abilities for God's glory. "Each of you should use whatever gift you have received to serve others, as faithful stewards of God's grace in its various forms" (1 Peter 4, NIV). Serve others with your skills through volunteering, mentoring, or actively participating in your local church. Seek opportunities to develop and grow your talents. Be open to using them in new and creative ways.

Meaningful Relationships

Invest in meaningful relationships with others. Practice active listening, empathy, and support for those around you. Encourage others in their faith and help them grow spiritually. Foster an environment of love, grace, and forgiveness in your relationships. In all your relationship endeavors, always remember that "Bad company corrupts good character, so do not be misled" (1 Corinthians 15:33).

Care for Creation

As followers of Christ, God has entrusted us with the responsibility of caring for the earth. We must acknowledge that we do not own the earth, but rather, it belongs to the Lord, as stated in Psalm 24:1. Therefore, we must also act as responsible stewards of the environment and ensure that we preserve it for future generations. Our role as caretakers of God's creation is highlighted in Genesis 2:15, where we are instructed to tend to the earth. Our uses of the earth's resources must be designed to conserve and renew them rather than deplete or destroy them. Our goal as Christians is to honor God by caring for His creation. By recognizing our role as caretakers of the earth and actively seeking ways to promote sustainability, we can fulfill our responsibility as good stewards of God's creation.

Knowledge and Education

Continually seek knowledge and grow your understanding of God and His Word. Engage in lifelong learning, reading Christian literature, attending seminars or conferences, and participating in Bible studies or discipleship programs. Use your knowledge to teach and share with others.

Health and Self-Care

Our overall health is an indispensable aspect of our well-being. Taking care of our well-being is integral to living a fulfilling life. In 1 Corinthians 6:19-20, Paul emphasizes that our physical body is a temple of the Holy Spirit. Therefore, we should take good care of our physical, mental, emotional, and spiritual health. To maintain good physical health, we should exercise regularly, get sufficient rest, and nourish ourselves with nutritious food.

In addition to health, consider prioritizing your mental and emotional well-being. Proverbs 17:22 says, "A cheerful heart is a good medicine, but a crushed spirit dries up the bones." This passage accentuates the significance of maintaining a positive mental attitude and finding peace and joy in life. Preventing burnout and promoting emotional resilience can be achieved by practicing self-care, including engaging in relaxing activities and building a support system with loved ones.

Above all, we must take care of our spiritual health. This can involve practicing prayer, meditation, or other forms of spiritual reflection. Matthew 6:33 reminds us to aim for the kingdom of God and His righteousness, as God will add everything else to us. Prioritizing our relationship with God can help us find peace and purpose. Following biblical principles and self-care can stimulate us to better serve others and honor God with our bodies and minds.

Prayer and Seeking God's Guidance

Regularly seek God's guidance in all areas of life. Pray for wisdom and discernment in stewarding your resources, making decisions, and discerning His will. Cultivate a habit of seeking God's guidance through prayer and surrendering your plans and desires to Him. Remember that being a good steward is a lifelong journey and requires ongoing intentional devotion. It involves continually seeking God's guidance, being accountable, and making choices that align with His principles. By practicing good stewardship, you can effectively use your resources and talents to positively impact the world and bring glory to God.

Be A Good Steward Of Your Profession

Faith does not excuse competence and integrity. Know how to do your job and do it well, as only your best is ever good enough. It is essential to recognize that the work of your hand is a gift from God. It is also a means to serve Him and others. Being a good steward of your profession means acknowledging that your work is not just a means to earn a living but also an opportunity to use your gifts and talents for the glory of God. Strive to work diligently and excellently in your profession. Use your skills, talents, and abilities, and consistently seek to bring honor to God through the quality of your work and your commitment to doing it well. Do not forget that you are called to work with all your heart as if you are working for the Lord, not for human masters, and to do so with excellence and integrity. Maintain high integrity and ethical standards in your profession. Seek to live out biblical values and principles, even when faced with dilemmas. Let your character and conduct in the workplace testify to your faith in Christ.

Service and Influence

Use your position and influence to promote justice, fairness, and compassion in your workplace. Seek to meet the necessities of those you serve, whether they are colleagues, clients, customers, or the broader community impacted by your work. If you occupy a leadership role, consider it an opportunity to lead with humility, grace, and servant-heartedness. Understand that you do not have to be in a leadership role, rank, or position to lead others. You can always lead by influence regardless of your status. Seek to mentor and develop others, investing in their growth and well-being. Use your influence to foster a healthy and supportive work environment that sustains an atmosphere for progression.

Faith Integration

Look for ways to integrate your faith into your professional life. This may require you to align your values and beliefs with your work. It may also require ethical decisions considering the broader impact of your actions. Pray for wisdom and discernment in navigating work-related challenges, conflicts, and decisions. Maintain a kingdom perspective in your profession. Recognize that your work is not just a means to earn a living but an opportunity to participate in God's redemptive work. Seek to bring God's love, truth, and transformation to your workplace and industry by being a light in a world that needs it.

When you approach your work in this way, you will not only be fulfilling your duties as an employee but also be a witness to others of the love and grace of God. You will be able to serve others compassionately, meet their needs, and build relationships that can lead to opportunities to share the gospel. Remember that you will receive a reward from the Lord for your excellent work and that it is the Christ you serve. So, whether you are a doctor, a teacher, a business owner, or any other professional, use your skills and talents to serve God and others and strive to be the best you can be as God empowers you.

For Reflection

1. Which areas of your life do you need to be more mindful of to be a good steward?

2. The quote, "Faith does not excuse competence and integrity. Know how to do your job and do it well, as only your best is ever good enough," highlights the importance of being competent and maintaining integrity in your work. What are your thoughts on this statement?

3. Let's consider the potential obstacles to being a good steward. How might these challenges manifest in your life? What strategies could you employ to overcome them?

4. How could you track your progress in becoming a better steward? And, importantly, how might you engage others in your journey?

5. How have you utilized your skills, resources, and time to impact the people and places in your community?

6. Could you share specific instances where you took action to help those around you?

Food For Thought

For the moment, all discipline seems painful rather than pleasant, but later, it yields the peaceful fruit of righteousness to those who have been trained by it.

Hebrews 12:11

Twelve

A DISCIPLE IS SPIRITUALLY DISCIPLINED

> *Discipline yourself for the purpose of godliness.*
>
> **1 Timothy 4:7, NASB**

Spirituality is one of the most frequently used words today, popping up in different contexts and organizations and with different connotations. As Christians, we should not just talk about spirituality; we should seek true, Christ-centered spirituality. According to Michael A. G. Haykin, author of The God Who Draws Near, true spirituality is bound up with the Holy Spirit and His work.[1] True spirituality means living a life by the Holy Spirit. It means being in God and God being in the believer. Is this not the essence of the Christian life? Is this not how we should live our lives as Christians? True spirituality, which is intimately bound up with the Holy Spirit, means to live in harmony with the Holy Spirit.[2]

Living under the Spirit's leadership demands that we practice spiritual disciplines to stay in tune with God. In this chapter, I will help you start by presenting some critical aspects of being spiritually disciplined and cultivating a disciplined mind for godliness.

This Holy Spirit enables believers from all walks of life to be faithful followers of Christ. As much as we allow the Holy Spirit through spiritual disciplines, we can obey God's Word daily. The spiritual disciplines help believers grow in Christ and prioritize spiritual formation. What are spiritual disciplines? Whitney defines spiritual disciplines as practices in Scripture that promote spiritual growth among believers in the gospel of Jesus Christ.[3] This means exercising our body, spirit, and soul for godliness as our utmost priority. Let us discuss what it means for Christians to discipline themselves.

Spiritual Disciplines as a Means of Godliness

Godliness is a critical component of the Christian faith. It involves living a holy life, which is vital for our spiritual journey and relationship with God. Hebrews 12:14 advises us to pursue peace with everyone and to achieve godliness because we cannot see the Lord without it. Practicing the spiritual disciplines is the way to cultivate godliness. These practices are essential for our spiritual formation and help us deepen our relationship with God. With the Holy Spirit's guidance, we can incorporate spiritual disciplines into our daily lives and become more godly.

These disciplines help us become more Christlike. They also lead us to spiritual maturity. Discipline is essential in promoting spiritual growth among believers. It is not enough for us to wait for holiness to come to us; we must pursue it. The Apostle Paul emphasizes this in 1 Timothy 4:8, stating that godliness has value for all things and that we should train ourselves for godliness. This training requires discipline, which is necessary to attain holiness as we strive to be like Christ. It holds the promise for the present and future life. We are charged with training ourselves for godliness. Through this discipline, we can grow and mature in our faith. Pursuing spiritual discipline can make us more like Jesus and fulfill God's calling. Later in this chapter, we will delve deeper into the teachings of the Apostle Paul regarding spiritual discipline and its importance.

The Bible offers numerous spiritual disciplines that help Christians grow and mature in their faith with the Holy Spirit's guidance. While Whitney emphasizes spiritual disciplines as activities only found in the Bible, the Bible itself does not limit how we discipline ourselves for godliness's sake. Although spiritual disciplines are practices, they cannot be isolated from our character qualities, attitude, or the fruit of the Spirit, as described in Galatians 5:22–23. Without these traits, practicing the spiritual disciplines is impossible. Practicing the spiritual disciplines without exhibiting the fruit of the spirit is useless.

Practicing spiritual disciplines is reflected in various actions, including reading, meditating, praying, fasting, worshiping, serving, and learning. These disciplines require consistent effort as they help us to mature in our faith and become more like Christ. For example, reading the Bible helps us gain knowledge of God's character, while meditation helps us internalize and apply what we've learned. Prayer is a means of communicating with God and growing in our relationship with Him, while fasting helps us focus on God and His will. Worshiping God allows us to express our love and adoration for Him while serving others, reflecting Christ's love and compassion for humanity. Learning helps us gain wisdom and knowledge, which we can apply and share with others.

Spiritual disciplines can be perceived by others in how they are reflected in our attitude and character and how we portray the fruit of the Spirit. Timothy was charged to discipline himself for the purpose of godliness, which meant his life needed to be spiritually formed to conform to Christ. Becoming more like Jesus in our words and actions is the main reason for beginning any spiritual discipline. As Whitney argues, it is not our pursuit of holiness that qualifies us to see the Lord. Instead, God Himself qualifies us to see Him. Our human or sinful nature means there is no way we can generate enough righteousness to influence God and earn admittance into heaven. God has given His only begotten Son, Jesus, who lived a life good enough to be accepted by God and worthy of entrance into heaven. In Jesus, we have the grace to be righteous and redeemed by Him. Therefore, we don't need to work to qualify for redemptive grace, but we are encouraged to mature in faith, which will naturally lead to good works.

Spiritual disciplines, such as prayer, fasting, Bible study, meditation, and solitude, can help us grow in our faith and become more like Christ. However, not the disciplines themselves save us or make us holy; they are tools that draw us closer to God. As we allow the Holy Spirit to work in us through these disciplines, we can experience transformation and maturity. Maturing in faith is also known as working out our salvation. As Philippians 2:12 (paraphrased) says, "Continue to work out your salvation with fear and trembling. Remember that God works within you, helping you desire and act according to His good purposes." This passage encourages us to live in a way that reflects Christ. This means living in harmony with acts of trust, faith, love, confidence, joy, and humility instead of self-satisfaction. This passage also urges us to live a life of perpetual obedience to God's Word in total humility, without relying on our works or vain praise but continually crediting it solely to God's grace. Becoming a spiritually disciplined disciple is not easy; it requires intentional effort and practice.

To achieve spiritual discipline, we must cultivate spiritual habits and disciplines that promote growth, maturity, and intimacy with God. These spiritual habits include prayer, fasting, meditation, Bible study, attending worship services, serving others, and practicing forgiveness. To grow spiritually, we must align our lives with Jesus's teachings. Spiritual disciplines are not legalistic rituals but a pathway to encountering God, growing in faith, and experiencing His transformative power. They are not a one-time event or a quick fix but a lifelong pursuit that requires dedication, commitment, and patience. Here are some critical aspects of being spiritually disciplined.

Habitual Prayer Life

In 1 Thessalonians 5:17–18, the Apostle Paul encourages us to pray constantly while giving thanks in all circumstances since it is God's will for them in Christ Jesus. A habitual prayer life is an essential discipline. It requires consistent and meaningful communication with God in private and public settings. Disciples must dedicate time to praying, expressing gratitude, seeking guidance, confessing sins, and interceding for others.

Fasting, Abstaining, and Sacrificing

Fasting, abstaining, and sacrificing are spiritual practices that people have followed for centuries across various religions and cultures. Fasting typically involves refraining from food or certain activities for a specific period. This practice is meant to enhance spiritual focus and self-discipline and has been found to have numerous health benefits. In some religions or denominations, fasting is observed during specific times of the year or season, such as the beginning or end of the year or Lent in Christianity. During this time, people often commit to abstaining from certain foods or activities to purify themselves and strengthen their spiritual connection.

Abstaining is a spiritual discipline that goes beyond simply avoiding food. It encompasses avoiding specific behaviors or indulgences or engaging in certain activities. By abstaining from these things, individuals can develop greater self-control and cultivate a deeper connection with their beliefs. This practice is often combined with fasting and other spiritual practices and can help strengthen your spiritual and mental well-being. In a spiritual context, sacrificing involves giving up something valuable as an offering or a symbol of devotion. It is often aimed at spiritual purification and humility. Sacrificing can take various forms, depending on the religion or culture. In Christianity, it can be the act of giving to charities or doing volunteer work. It can also be donating money to people experiencing poverty or resources to those in need.

These practices strengthen your connection with your beliefs, promote self-discipline, and showcase devotion to a greater purpose. Additionally, they can positively affect your health, such as enhancing digestion, decreasing inflammation, and improving the immune system. Ultimately, these practices help us develop inner peace and spiritual contentment.

Biblical Fasting

Scripturally, fasting is a spiritual discipline that involves abstaining from food and using that time to focus on God, seek His guidance, and cultivate self-discipline. Fasting has been observed by many people of faith throughout history as a way of drawing closer to God and seeking His will. Scriptural fasting is not just about refraining from food; it is a time dedicated to worshipping and reflecting on your relationship with God. It is a time to pray, meditate, and seek spiritual renewal. By denying yourself the physical pleasure of food, you can become more attuned to the spiritual realm and more receptive to God's guidance.

Fasting is not a ritual or charm, nor a way to gain God's favor or manipulate Him into doing what we want. Instead, it is a humble acknowledgment of our dependence on God and a way of expressing our desire to seek His will above ours. Fasting is an act of worship that teaches us to trust God profoundly and become more obedient to His leadership. This practice deepens our faith and strengthens our relationship with God.

The passage in Matthew 6:16-18 provides detailed instructions from Jesus on how to fast in a way pleasing to God. He advises that when you fast, you should not put on a downcast face as the hypocrites do, for they seek to draw attention to themselves and their piety. Instead, Jesus suggests that you anoint your head and wash your face so that you look fresh and clean and others do not notice your fasting.

By doing this, Jesus explains that your fasting will be for God's eyes only and not for the admiration of others. This selfless approach to fasting will bring you closer to God, and He will reward you accordingly. The rewards of fasting are not earthly but spiritual and come from knowing that you have pleased God by following His commandments. So, as you fast, remember to focus on God and the spiritual rewards that come from following His word rather than seeking the approval of others.

Bible Study and Meditation

Engaging in Bible study and meditation is crucial to building spiritual discipline. By dedicating time to studying and reflecting on God's Word, we can deeply understand its meaning and relevance to our lives. As we meditate on Scripture, we allow its teachings to become ingrained in our hearts and minds, shaping our thoughts, attitudes, and actions. Bible study involves delving into Scripture, examining its historical and cultural context, and analyzing its meaning.

Meditation involves quiet reflection on the Scriptures, allowing their wisdom to penetrate our hearts and minds. These practices can deepen our relationship with God as we seek to live out His will with the knowledge of the Holy Bible. Whether through individual or group discussions, Bible study and meditation are powerful tools for spiritual growth.

Worship

"God is a spirit, and as His worshipers, you must worship Him in the spirit and in truth" (Jn 4:24). This statement reminds us that worship is about connecting with God on a deep, spiritual level. It calls us to be authentic and to seek a genuine relationship with our Creator. Worship is crucial to our spiritual growth and discipleship. It involves expressing our love and gratitude and surrendering to God. Personal worship is an individual experience that can take many forms, such as singing, praying, or reading Scripture. By engaging in these practices, we can connect with God and grow our relationship with Him. Corporate worship refers to coming together with other believers to worship God. This can occur in a church, a small group, or any other setting where believers gather.

Corporate worship has a way of thrusting us into the communal power of God's presence. A sincere heart of worship is paramount to this holy experience. This involves dedicating daily time to personal worship, such as reading devotional materials or listening to worship music. This strengthens our bond with God and enhances our spiritual growth. Participating in corporate worship gatherings helps us experience the power of community and deepen our connection with God.

Sabbath Rest and Self-care

Sabbath rest is a spiritual discipline that encourages us to embrace regular periods of rest and renewal. It involves setting aside a day or specific times for rest, reflection, and reconnecting with God. This discipline is not just about taking time off from work or avoiding certain activities; it is about creating space for God to work in our lives and to refresh our spirits. Engaging in activities that help us connect with God and ourselves during this time is essential. This could be praying, reading the Bible, meditating, or simply enjoying nature. By doing so, we will develop a more profound sense of our spiritual journey and feel more connected to our purpose in life.

Sabbath rest is not just a day of the week to relax. It's an opportunity to revitalize our spiritual, mental, physical, and emotional batteries. It allows us to prioritize self-care, reflect on what matters in life, and cultivate relationships, health, and personal growth. By making sabbath rest a regular part of our lives, we will accomplish a more balanced, spiritually, and emotionally fulfilling life.

Community and Fellowship

Building a robust community and fostering fellowship with other believers is crucial for spiritual growth. Engaging in meaningful relationships through small groups, attending church services, and developing deep connections with fellow disciples provides a platform for accountability, encouragement, and support in your spiritual journey.

Participating in small groups allows you to connect with others who share your faith and interests. In a supportive and safe atmosphere, you can ask questions, share your experiences, and learn from others. Attending church services allows you to worship with others, hear inspiring messages, and receive guidance from spiritual leaders. Developing deep connections with fellow disciples is essential for building a solid support system. These relationships provide accountability, encouragement, and support in your spiritual walk. You can find comfort in sharing your victories and struggles, knowing you're not alone on your journey, and you can pray for one another.

Self-examination and Confession

Self-examination and confession are critical biblical spiritual disciplines that can transform your life and improve your relationship with God. Discipleship requires regular examination of one's heart, motives, and actions in light of God's truth. It involves stepping back from our busy lives and asking ourselves probing questions such as, "Am I living under God's will?" or "Am I treating my neighbors as I would like to be treated?" By reflecting on our actions, thoughts, and attitudes, we can recognize any sins of disobedience that may hamper our relationship with God.

Confession is another crucial aspect of this discipline. We may find that we have fallen short of God's expectations as we examine our lives. In these moments, we must humbly confess our sins and disobedience to God and ask for His forgiveness and restoration. Confession is acknowledging our wrongdoings, taking responsibility, and seeking to make things right with those we have wronged. Allowing the Holy Spirit to convict us of our sins results in transformation and empowers us to live a life that is pleasing to God. Self-examination and confession are not one-time events but continuous processes requiring discipline and commitment.

Service and Acts of Compassion

This spiritual discipline demonstrates Christ's love and compassion by engaging in acts of kindness, mercy, and justice, reflecting God's heart for the broken and the marginalized.

Service involves meeting the needs of others and putting their well-being before our own. It can take many forms, from volunteering at a local charity to helping a neighbor with yard work. Acts of compassion involve showing kindness and empathy to those hurting physically, emotionally, or spiritually. We can always follow in the footsteps of Jesus, who spent His entire life serving others and demonstrating God's love and compassion. By engaging in acts of service and compassion, we follow Christ's example and help bring hope and healing to a hurting world.

Disciplined Mind and Thoughts

This spiritual discipline requires us to guard our minds against negative influences and unhealthy thought patterns. As disciples, we must renew our minds with God's truth and choose to dwell on pure, true, noble, and praiseworthy things. Having a disciplined mind means being aware of our thoughts and emotions and examining them in light of the truth of God's Word. We must learn to recognize negative patterns and replace them with positive ones. When we focus on the things that are pure, true, noble, and praiseworthy, our minds become more apparent and our hearts more peaceful.

Cultivating a disciplined mind and thoughts requires aligning our thoughts with God's Word and allowing the Holy Spirit to transform us from the inside out.

Submission

Submission is a spiritual discipline that requires surrendering your desires and priorities to align with God's plan. Submission is not a passive act but an active choice to follow God's guidance and direction in all areas of life. Biblically, submission is a crucial aspect of living as a follower of Christ. This means submitting to God's authority and resisting the devil's temptations, as we are instructed in James 4:7. In Ephesians 5:21, we are called to submit to one another to prioritize the needs and desires of others above our own. This command is grounded in our reverence for Christ and His example of selfless love. Furthermore, Romans 13:1 reminds us that God establishes all governing authorities; therefore, we should submit to their leadership and laws. By submitting to God and others, we can cultivate a spirit of humility and service that reflects the heart of Christ.

Practicing submission means acknowledging God as our ultimate authority. It involves humbly accepting His will and trusting His good plans for us. Submission also requires letting go of our ambitions and desires and seeking God's will above all else. This can be challenging, as our natural tendency is to prioritize our interests and desires. However, through submission, we can learn to trust God's plan and find peace and contentment in His guidance. Submission is not a one-time event but a continuous practice that requires discipline and commitment. It involves consistently seeking God's guidance, remaining in prayer, and studying the Bible to understand His will. Ultimately, practicing submission is an act of worship, demonstrating our love and obedience to God.

The Apostle Paul on Spiritual Discipline

First, Timothy 4:7–8 guides personal spiritual discipline and training in godliness. In this passage, the Apostle Paul cautions his young disciple, Timothy, to avoid getting caught up in false teachings or speculative ideas that lack reverence for God and do not contribute to spiritual growth. Instead, Paul encourages Timothy to focus on training himself in godliness. The phrase "irreverent and silly myths" refers to false teachings or religious traditions that may have been prevalent during that time. These myths could have been distractions or sources of confusion that hindered the pursuit of genuine faith and godliness. Paul advises Timothy to avoid such beliefs and not invest time or energy into them but to focus instead on the essential teachings of the faith.

Paul emphasizes the importance of spiritual discipline when he urges believers to develop a Christ-centered character, cultivate virtues and qualities that reflect God's nature, and align their lives with God's will. This is more than just acquiring knowledge and intellectual understanding. It is an intense pursuit of devotion to God. This passage reminds believers to prioritize spiritual growth and invest in disciplines such as prayer, studying Scripture, worship, and following the example of Jesus Christ. By training yourself in godliness, you can deepen your relationship with God and bear the fruit of a transformed life.

In addition, Paul highlights the value of physical training, recognizing its benefits for the present life. However, he emphasizes that godliness has value for all things, holding promise for both the present life and the life to come. Pursuing godliness leads to a life of purpose and fulfillment in this world and the hereafter. By practicing these habits consistently, you can develop an unwavering rhythm of spiritual practices that nurtures your soul and deepens your relationship with God. Spiritual discipline can be challenging, but it produces a closer relationship with God, a more profound sense of purpose, and a more fulfilling life.

Notes

[1] Michael A. G. Haykin, The God Who Draws Near: An Introduction to Biblical Spirituality (Webster, NY: Evangelical Press, 2007), 2.

[2] Ibid, 22.

[3] Donald S. Whitney, Spiritual Disciplines for the Christian Life, revised ed. (Colorado Springs, CO: NavPress, 2014), 4.

For Reflection

1. We have discussed how God uses spiritual disciplines to grow us in godliness. Seize this moment to meditate, pray, and reflect upon which disciplines God wants you to utilize more faithfully to grow in godliness.

2. How do you plan to be more faithful in practicing these disciplines? Could you be specific and practical in your plan?

3. What aspects of Christianity make it a challenging faith to follow?

4. Since Revelation 12:11a assures us that we can overcome the devil through the blood of the Lamb and by our testimony, will you commit to sharing your plan with at least three people this week?

Notes

Section Three

ASSESSMENTS

Thirteen

ASSESSMENT

The Essential Marks of a True Disciple

> *Examine yourselves to see if your faith is genuine. Test your-*
> *selves. Surely, you know that Jesus Christ is among you; if*
> *not, you have failed the test of authentic faith.*
>
> **2 Corinthians 13:5**

As you reach the end of the first two sections of this book, it's natural to wonder how you are progressing in your journey as a disciple. Are you curious about where you currently stand and where to improve? If so, there is a helpful spiritual assessment that you can use to evaluate yourself more closely through the lens of the Bible.

This assessment is not a test to determine whether you are a disciple. Rather, it is a tool designed specifically to help you identify areas where you need to work to grow as a disciple. By assessing the specific characteristics of a disciple, you can get a clear and honest picture of your spiritual trajectory. The assessment will help you to identify areas where you are already healthy and strong and where you need to focus your attention to improve. It's an excellent way to evaluate yourself and refine your spiritual growth. So, this assessment is a great place to start if you want to develop a more profound understanding of your spiritual journey.

As we proceed in this book, it would be worthwhile to take some time to introspect and evaluate the genuineness of our faith. Testing ourselves helps us better understand the presence of Christ within us and the extent to which we have succeeded or fallen short in demonstrating authentic faith. So, it is time to get your pen and begin your assessment on the next page.

Mark 1 - Obedience

Mark 1 A Disciple is Obedient	Always	Occasionally	Not Sure	Sometimes	Never
	4	3	2	1	0
1. I submit my body as a temple of Christ through scripture, self-discipline, and exercise to keep me holy and acceptable.					
2. I concern myself more with God's will and approval than the approval of men, women, leaders, or others in everything I do.					
3. I acknowledge the lordship of Christ and His will in all my ways.					
4. I consistently show my total obedience to God through my words, attitudes, and actions in everything I do, even when no one is looking.					
5. Following through with the Great Commission in Matthew 28:19–20, I must first obey the commandment before I can teach it to others.					
6. I attempt to obey all aspects of God's will, even those that are difficult to embrace.					
7. I worship God and pray on a regular basis and spend time listening to where He is leading me.					
Total Point Value For Each Response:					
Add and enter all point values:					
Divide total point value by 2:					
Final total point value for mark 1:					

Mark 2 - Mission

Mark 2 **A Disciple is Missional**	Always	Occasionally	Not Sure	Sometimes	Never
	4	3	2	1	0
1. Following Christ means His mission becomes my mission.					
2. I am, or I desire to be, involved in local or foreign outreach programs (missions) led by the church or ministry to which I belong.					
3. I am very concerned for the lost people (unbelievers), and I am motivated to invite them to Christ.					
4. Each day, I live in such a way that my life, words, attitude, and actions testify that I am a Christian and draw those around me to Christ.					
5. The Great Commission in Matthew 28:19–20 dominates my mind daily.					
6. I make my faith known to my neighbors and/or fellow employees.					
7. I share my faith in Christ with non-believers.					
Total point value for each response:					
Add and enter all point values:					
Divide total point value by 2:					
Total point value for mark 2					

Mark 3 - Community

Mark 3 A Disciple is Communal	Always	Occasionally	Not Sure	Sometimes	Never
	4	3	2	1	0
1. I serve, or I am serving, a body of believers, group, or the Church of God with my God-given gifts regularly.					
2. I show my devotion to God by loving and connecting with people.					
3. I find my true identity in Christ as I engage in God's mission with the church/community of faith.					
4. I turn the other cheek when I am hurt, insulted, or attacked by others, and I forgive them whether they ask for forgiveness or not.					
5. I pray and intercede for other believers, spiritual leaders, and the Church as a whole.					
6. My time commitments demonstrate that I value relationships over work, career, and hobbies.					
7. I admit errors in my relationships and seek forgiveness from those whom I have hurt.					
Total point value for each response:					
Add and enter all point values:					
Divide total point value by 2:					
Total point value for mark 3:					

Mark 4 - Humility & Servanthood

Mark 4 A Disciple is a Humble Servant	Always	Occasionally	Not Sure	Sometimes	Never
	4	3	2	1	0
1. Serving in positions below my status or title excites me.					
2. I feel fulfilled when I can serve in an area of need.					
3. I prefer a stable relationship or a long-term relationship in which I can model humility and servanthood for new converts or growing believers.					
4. I serve members and non-members of our church, group, or fellowship.					
5. I regularly utilize my God-given spiritual gift(s) to build up others in a small group or church for mutual support, encouragement, uplifting even without recognition.					
6. I allow other Christians to hold me accountable for spiritual growth.					
7. I encourage and listen to feedback from others to help me discover areas for spiritual formation and growth.					
Total point value for each response:					
Add and enter all point values:					
Divide total point value by 2:					
Total point value for mark 4:					

Mark 5 - Multiplication

Mark 5 A Disciple is a Multiplier	Always	Occasionally	Not Sure	Sometimes	Never
	4	3	2	1	0
1. I am nurturing the spiritual lives of others, sharing my faith story, offering spiritual encouragement, and leading others to Christ to fulfill their calling as disciples.					
2. I carry out Jesus's command in Matthew 28:18–20.					
3. I believe that I have the ability and the characteristics embedded in me to be a multiplier of the gospel of Christ.					
4. I am committed to nurture and disciple others so that the multiplication process continues.					
5. I am an integral part of the Church, called to train and deploy disciples (Mt 28:19–20).					
6. I make sure the people I witness to get the follow-up and support they need to grow in Christ.					
7. My actions demonstrate a belief in and commitment to the Great Commission (Mt 28:19–20).					
Total point value for each response:					
Add and enter all point values:					
Divide total point value by 2:					
Final total point value for mark 5:					

Mark 6 - Stewardship

Mark 6 A Disciple is a Good Steward	Always	Occasionally	Not Sure	Sometimes	Never
	4	3	2	1	0
1. I sacrificially contribute a considerable amount of my finances, time, resources to help others in need in my church and faith community.					
2. I regularly contribute time to a ministry at my church.					
3. I organize and plan the use of my time and money carefully.					
4. I enjoy a meaningful time with God through Bible reading and prayer each day.					
5. I regularly give at least one tenth of my income toward God's work.					
6. I reduce, reuse, and recycle products.					
7. I manage my time effectively.					
Total point value for each response:					
Add and enter all point values:					
Divide total point values by 2:					
Final total point value for mark 6:					

Mark 7 - Spiritual Discipline

Mark 7 A Disciple is Spiritually Disciplined	Always 4	Occasionally 3	Not Sure 2	Sometimes 1	Never 0
1. I practice a regular quiet time and look forward to that time with Christ.					
2. Generally, my public and private self are the same.					
3. I evaluate cultural ideas, trends, and lifestyles by biblical standards first.					
4. As a means of growing in Christ, I prayerfully practice various spiritual disciplines.					
5. I have clear boundaries and avoid temptation at all costs. I cannot remember the last time I crossed a path I shouldn't have.					
6. I listen more than I talk and listen with a desire to understand. I use my words as a source of encouragement and love.					
7. My values guide my attitudes, decisions, and actions.					
Total point value for each response:					
Add and enter all point values:					
Divide total point value by 2:					
Final total point value for mark 7:					

Summary

Summary of Marks	My Total Value	Highest Value	Lowest Value
Mark 1		14	0
Mark 2		14	0
Mark 3		14	0
Mark 4:		14	0
Mark 5		14	0
Mark 6		14	0
Mark 7		14	0
YOUR FINAL SCORE (add all of your marks)		98	0

Comments

Score	Comments
0 – 24	You have answered the call and are still taking some baby steps and making progress in some areas. It would be best to have some nurturing and mentoring to help you become a good disciple. You may be a new convert or a Christian just starting out. At this stage, you still need to improve in one area or the other and need more scriptural understanding and mentorship. Jesus is calling you to follow Him more closely. You must ask yourself, are you prepared to answer and follow Christ's call to discipleship?

25 – 49

You have made good progress following Christ to this level, but perhaps you are still struggling in some areas of your life, possibly grappling with some part of the Bible. While it can be challenging to let go, it is fundamental to our spiritual growth. Studying more about Jesus and His teachings will help you take the needed step of faith anytime you doubt.

50 – 74

You have worked well with the help of the Holy Spirit to get to this level. Like Jesus's disciples, you still find some of Jesus's teachings hard to understand. You are on the right path as a disciple of Jesus, but don't stop here! There are still significant areas of learning ahead. Remember, as a disciple, you are always learning and growing.

74–98

You are intentional about Jesus's command in Matthew 28:18–20. You have embraced the leverage from building capacity for disciple-making through the multiplication of healthy and reproducing believers. Through the Holy Spirit, you exercise the knowledge, ability, and characteristics embedded in you to reproduce. Others can see that you are a faithful follower of Christ. The essential marks of a disciple (obedience, mission, community, humble servanthood, multiplication, good steward, and spiritual discipline) are growing in you as you follow Christ. Don't get too comfortable, though, because a disciple's transformation is an ongoing and unending process of spiritual formation where the Holy Spirit works in your life as you carry out the Great Commission.

Fourteen

ANALYSIS OF ASSESSMENT RESULTS

> *Test yourselves to see if your faith is genuine. Surely, you know that Jesus Christ is among you. If not, you have failed the test of genuine faith.*
>
> **2 Corinthians 13:5**

In this segment, we will describe, summarize, and analyze the results of this self-assessment in a way that will show where an assessed individual is healthy and where maturity is needed. This assessment evaluates growth areas based on the seven marks of a disciple: obedience, mission, community, humility, multiplication, stewardship, and practicing the spiritual disciplines. It is not designed to determine whether you are a disciple. It is only meant to help you figure out areas that require work. This assessment is one of the ways we can evaluate a believer's spiritual formation. This assessment shows where you are strong and healthy and where you need to discipline yourself for the purpose of godliness, especially in these seven marks of a disciple.

Since obedience is the primary response to the call to discipleship, the assessment begins with the disciple's first mark. Obedience influences the quality of experience for missional discipleship. Van Gelder and Zscheile argue that as disciples obey God's Word, the Holy Spirit continues to conform them to the image of Christ.[1] Furthermore, through His life and actions, even unto death on the cross, Jesus exemplified this mark of discipleship by His complete obedience to the Father (Phil 2:8). When we claim to follow Christ, it means we are committed to spiritual disciplines teach us to obey God in totality. Christian spiritual formation in the missional movement has at its core conformity to the example and person of Christ through continual obedience.[2]

The following assessment area is that of mission, as the second mark of discipleship is being missional. Maddix argues that discipleship is spiritual formation, Christian nurturing, and mentoring, including compassionate service and missional engagement.[3] Through these acts of discipleship, disciples are shaped and formed as they mature and grow in grace through various spiritual disciplines. Frost and Hirsch also argued that discipleship's essential task is to equip believers to embody the message of Jesus.[4] Through this missional mark of discipleship, believers can find an authentic and God-intended identity as they engage in God's mission with the faith community.[5] Although the mission is an expectation of a disciple, being missional is critical for a disciple's spiritual formation. This is why we must assess this area of discipleship.

The third assessment area is how a disciple functions in faith communities, as the third mark of discipleship is being communal. This assessment area helps disciples evaluate their roles and relationships in the faith community. It also equips leaders to identify

contradictions to the communal mark or characteristics of discipleship to encourage shared spiritual-formation practices for the purpose of godliness. In Paul's time, Gorman argues that the ekklēsia
was not an optional supplement to a private spirituality of dying
and rising with Christ.[6] Hirsch agrees that the faith community
is fundamental for shaping the disciple's identity, as it becomes a
context of transformative experience.[7] Halter and Smay argue that
a Christian or a faith community was very intriguing, unique, and
attractive primarily because it called for all people's inclusion.[8] The
testimony of this mark in a disciple's life or the lack of this mark in
a disciple's life will help evaluate the believer's spiritual formation.
As a spiritual discipline, this is where prayer is needed, as we
are encouraged in Colossians 4:2 to continue steadfastly in prayer.
Whitney reminds us that God expects Christians to be devoted to
prayer.[9]

The fourth assessment area is how a disciple functions as a humble servant (Luke 9:14–17). Humble service is critical to discipleship
and the spiritual formation of a believer. Servanthood and humility
go hand in hand. One cannot serve with pride and arrogance, which
are unacceptable for any form of discipleship. Jesus exemplifies how
to be a humble disciple. He showed His heart for people by serving
His disciples while leading them to the discipline of servanthood.
The Apostle Paul often introduced himself as a servant, then an
apostle. He put his humility and servanthood before anything when
he wrote in Romans 1:1, "Paul, a servant of Christ Jesus, called to
be an apostle and set apart for the gospel of God."

This area of discipleship is assessed because one of the characteristics a disciple should be known for is being a humble servant
of Christ. Through a lifelong spiritual formation, disciples become
faithful servants of Christ. If you are a disciple but your life does
not reflect humility and servanthood, you may be caught up in
the pride of life. Murray argues that "the root and essence of all

Jesus's character as our redeemer is nothing but His humility."[10] Our humility is mainly seen through our service. The remarkable thing about being a disciple is that a disciple never stops learning, even if an assessment says you are 100 percent spiritually formed. The Great Commission in Matthew 28:19–20 can never be accomplished without total humility in service.

The fifth assessment area is how a disciple functions as a multiplier. Disciples take this mark from Christ and strive through the Holy Spirit's power to be a multiplier of His kingdom. Christ's disciples carried out the command in Matthew 28:18–20. Disciples embrace the leverage from building capacity for disciple-making by multiplying healthy, reproducing churches.[11] Each disciple should have the ability and the characteristics embedded in them to reproduce. The Apostle Paul charged Timothy to commit to faithful men who will also teach others (2 Tim 2:2). These faithful men and women should be equipped and dedicated to teaching others. Without this multiplication plan, it is challenging for the gospel to spread globally. If we can commit to reaching out to one person, disciple them, and charge them as Paul did to disciple others, the gospel will spread unfathomably. From Robert, we learn that multiplication becomes the fuel that grows the Church for future generations, although not as fast as most movements.[12] The only prospect for the faith community to grow is multiplication, which is also an avenue for spiritual formation. We must assess disciples in this area to see how they work toward populating God's kingdom.

The foundational strength of this essential mark is that we can believe that God has embedded the characteristics and ability to multiply in us. Through this assessment, we may discover that we need to learn how to better integrate ourselves into the missional practice of discipleship while being trained and deployed to witness and multiply.

The sixth assessment area is how a disciple functions as a good steward. This can help determine the extent of an individual's comprehension of the concept of stewardship. This includes assessing their ability to manage and utilize various resources such as finances, time, talents, and other assets. It can also identify areas where individuals may require further support or training to improve their stewardship practices. This might include developing financial literacy skills, learning to manage time more effectively, or enhancing their ability to serve others.

Finally, an assessment can help faith community leaders understand the overall culture of stewardship within their community and identify opportunities to promote and encourage good stewardship practices. This includes evaluating the effectiveness of existing programs and initiatives, identifying areas for improvement, and developing new strategies to foster a culture of good stewardship.

The seventh assessment area is how a disciple functions as a spiritually disciplined person. This exercise evaluates an individual's understanding and practice of the spiritual disciplines. It can help identify areas where individuals excel in their spiritual discipline practices and encourage them to continue their efforts. This assessment can also provide insights into areas where individuals may benefit from further support or training to improve their spiritual discipline practices. It presents an opportunity to offer guidance, resources, and encouragement to help individuals deepen their spiritual practices. It can also help faith leaders understand their community's overall culture of spiritual discipline and identify opportunities to promote and encourage spiritual discipline practices. This includes recognizing and celebrating the efforts of individuals who demonstrate solid spiritual discipline practices and developing new strategies to foster a culture of spiritual discipline that supports individuals' spiritual growth and development. Assessing this characteristic of a disciple helps individuals and faith community leaders work together to cultivate a constructive and supportive environment that encourages spiritual discipline practices and helps individuals deepen their relationship with God.

As Christians, we must seek true, Christ-centered spirituality. Practicing the spiritual disciplines matures us and ensures that spiritual formation is our top priority. Based on the spiritual assessment results, the personalized growth plan I provide supports growth in weak areas. Like Jesus's disciples, you still find some of Christ's teachings hard to understand. You are on the right path as a true disciple of Jesus, but you are encouraged to keep going. Don't stop here! Remember, this growth plan is just the beginning. There are still significant learning areas ahead of you. In addition to the growth plan and to help you learn and walk ever-growingly with Jesus, I provided further steps to help you stay closer to God in the following chapter.

Notes

[1] Craig Van Gelder and Dwight J. Zscheile, *The Missional Church in Perspective: Mapping Trends and Shaping the Conversation* (Grand Rapids, MI: Baker Academic, 2011), 89.

[2] Alan Hirsch and Debra Hirsch, *Untamed: Reactivating a Missional Form of Discipleship* (Grand Rapids, MI: Baker Books, 2010), 70.

[3] Mark A. Maddix, *Missional Discipleship: Partners in God's Redemptive Mission* (Kansas City, MO: Beacon Hill Press, 2013), 29.

[4] Alan Hirsch and Debra Hirsch, 70.

[5] Christopher Beard, "Missional Discipleship: Discerning Spiritual-Formation Practices and Goals Within the Missional Movement," *Missiology* 43, no. 2 (Apr 2015): 175–94.

[6] Michael J. Gorman, *Cruciformity: Paul's Narrative Spirituality of the Cross* (Grand Rapids, MI: Wm. B. Eerdmans Publishing Co., 2001), 367.

[7] Alan Hirsch and Debra Hirsch, 75.

[8] Hugh Halter and Matt Smay, *And: The Gathered and Scattered Church* (Exponential Series) (Grand Rapids: Zondervan, 2010), 120.

[9] Whitney, Donald S. *Spiritual Disciplines for the Christian Life* (Colorado Springs, CO: NavPress, 2014, 81).

[10] Andrew Murray, *Humility* (Nashville, TN: B&H Publishing Group, 2017), 24.

[11] Todd Wilson, *Multipliers: Leading Beyond Addition* (N.p.: United States Exponential, 2017), 55.

[12] Bob Roberts Jr., *The Multiplying Church: The New Math for Starting New Churches* (Grand Rapids: Zondervan, 2008), 61.

Fifteen

STEPS TO STAYING CLOSER TO GOD

> *Come close to God, and God will come close to you*
>
> **James 4:8**

1) Begin Each Day With Prayers

Beginning your day with prayer is a powerful way to recognize God's presence and show appreciation for His many blessings. For instance, you could start with a prayer of gratitude for the new day, strength and wisdom to confront the challenges ahead, and guidance in your decisions. Connecting with the Almighty can be a chance to seek His guidance, wisdom, and peace. These can all contribute to a sense of calm and reassurance lasting throughout your day.

As stated in Philippians 4:6-7, instead of worrying, we are encouraged to present our requests to God through prayer and petition, all while giving thanks. In doing so, the peace of God, which is beyond comprehension, will guard our hearts and minds through Christ. When you pray, doing more than asking for things is essential. Take the time to reflect on your life, your relationships, and your goals. Seek His guidance on navigating challenges and decisions you may face throughout the day. As you begin each day, commit it into God's hands, trusting Him for strength and direction. Remember that He is always with you, and His love and grace are sufficient to carry you through any situation. So, take a deep breath, bask in His presence, and let Him guide your steps throughout the day.

2) Read And Meditate on the Word

To enhance your relationship with God, abide by the words of the Psalmist: "Your word is a lamp to my feet and a light to my path" (Ps 119:105). One way to strengthen your spiritual life is allocating daily time to reading and meditating on the Scriptures. By 'meditate,' we mean to reflect on the meaning and implications of the verses deeply. Let them sink in, and allow them to guide your thoughts and actions. You may select a specific passage or theme to focus on, such as a Psalm of praise or a Gospel story, or follow a structured devotional plan that leads you through various parts of the Bible each day.

While reading, allow God's Word to touch your heart and guide your daily life. As Jesus Himself said, 'Humans cannot survive solely on bread, but they require every utterance that comes from the mouth of God to live' (Matt 4:4). Reflect on how these teachings apply to your unique circumstances and strive to implement God's principles in your everyday actions. This transformative process can inspire and motivate you, bringing joy and fulfillment to your spiritual journey.

By regularly engaging with God's Word in this way, you can deepen your spiritual understanding and grow in your relationship with Him. Remember to approach Scripture with an open heart and mind and seek the guidance of the Holy Spirit as you apply its teachings to your life. As the Apostle Paul wrote, "God has breathed out all Scripture, which is useful for teaching, reproofing, correcting, and training in righteousness"(2 Tim 3:16).

3) Talk to God

According to the Bible, communication with God is vital for developing a significant relationship with Him. 1 Thessalonians 5:17 encourages us to "pray without ceasing," which means maintaining a continuous conversation with God throughout the day. To achieve this, we must cultivate a spirit of dependence on God and invite Him into every aspect of our lives, including our decisions, relationships, and challenges. Proverbs 3:5-6 reminds us to trust the Lord completely and not rely on our understanding. Submit everything you do to him, and he will guide you on the right path.

We can share our joys, concerns, and struggles with God truthfully and transparently, with the assurance that He listens to and deeply cares for us. As mentioned in 1 Peter 5:7, we can unburden all our worries on Him because He cares for us. This form of communication with God can make us feel cherished and looked after, strengthening our relationship with Him and providing us with a deep sense of intimacy and solace. By cultivating a habit of communicating with God, we can enhance our relationship with Him and enjoy a closer connection to His presence and guidance in our daily lives. As we seek His will and place our trust in His provision, we can rest assured that He is always with us. As Jesus promised in Matthew 28:20, "And surely I am with you always, even to the end of the age."

4) Prayer Is Excellent, But Praise Is More Powerful

Prayer is a crucial part of our relationship with God as Christians. We are instructed by the Bible to offer our prayers continuously and to bring our concerns and desires to Him without ceasing (1 Thess 5:16-18). However, there are other ways to connect with God besides prayer. Along with prayer, the Bible emphasizes the importance of praise and thanksgiving. While prayer is a way to communicate with God, praise is a way to honor and acknowledge His greatness and faithfulness in our lives. According to Psalm 100:4, "Approach the gates of the Lord with a heart full of gratitude, and enter His courts with joyful adoration. Show your thankfulness to Him and lift His holy name in praise." When we praise God, we show our respect and honor to Him and enter His presence. We acknowledge His magnificence, faithfulness, and kindness in our lives.

Incorporating praise and thanksgiving into our daily routine is a powerful way to deepen our relationship with God. You can start your day by thanking God for the new day and His blessings and end your day by reflecting on the good things that happened and expressing gratitude. You can also sing hymns or praise songs that magnify His greatness, expressing gratitude for His faithfulness and blessings in our lives. As we do so, our spirits are uplifted, and our faith is strengthened.

When we praise God, we invite His presence into our lives. As we draw near to Him through praise and thanksgiving, we experience His love and grace in a new way. So, while prayer is excellent, praise is more powerful. By incorporating praise and thanksgiving into our daily routine, we honor God, uplift our spirits, and deepen our relationship with Him.

5) Take a Few Minutes to Be Quiet in the Lord's Presence

This process involves taking a few minutes to be still and quiet in the presence of the Lord. During this step, creating an environment free from distractions and noise is essential so that you can fully listen to God's voice. 'Being quiet in the Lord's presence' means being calm and open, ready to receive His guidance and peace. Practicing mindfulness in God's presence is recommended, allowing Him to speak to your heart and provide clarity and direction. You can accomplish this by concentrating on your body, breathing, and thoughts through the lens of the Holy Scriptures. As you spend time in quietness, be open to receiving God's insights, prompts, or revelations. These may come in any form: a still, small voice, a sense of His leading, a conviction, or a sudden realization or scriptural realization. It is vital to approach this time with an open heart, free from preconceived notions or expectations.

Remember that the Holy Spirit is always present and available to guide and direct you. By being still and listening, you are opening yourself to receive the wisdom and guidance only God can provide. So, take a few minutes to be quiet in the Lord's presence and allow Him to speak to your heart, giving you the clarity and direction you need.

6) Rest in God's Presence as the Day Draws to a Close

As the sun sets and another day comes to a close, it's essential to take a moment to reflect on God's faithfulness and goodness in your life. The book of Psalms says, "Giving thanks to the Lord is good, and singing praises to His name, O Most High, is also commendable. It is essential to declare His steadfast love in the morning and to acknowledge His faithfulness by night" (Ps 92:1-2). So, take a moment to review the day's events and recognize God's presence and guidance in every situation.

Express gratitude for His protection, provision, and answered prayers. Let us recall the message delivered by the apostle Paul, who advised us to steer clear of anxiety by presenting our requests to God through prayer and supplication with thanksgiving. By doing so, the peace of God that goes beyond our understanding guards your hearts and minds (Phil 4:6-7). Surrender any worries or burdens to God, trusting Him to carry them and provide rest for your soul. As you rest in God's presence, take comfort in the words of Jesus, who said, All of you who toil and bear heavy loads, come to me, and I will provide you with rest. Join me and learn from me, for I am kind and humble in heart, and you will find rest for your soul. My ways are easy, and my load is light (Matt 11:28-30). May you find peace and rest in God's loving arms as you gracefully end your day.

Following these steps regularly can establish a stronger and more profound connection with God. Dedicate time to prayer, study, and contemplate Scriptures, maintain constant communication with Him, express gratitude and appreciation, take moments of stillness to reflect, and meditate on God's unwavering loyalty. Doing so allows you to foster a closer relationship with Him and encounter His comforting presence and serenity in your daily life.

Greetings, my dear friends!

T hank you for the time you spent reading this book. I welcome you to new heights in your discipleship journey. Out of the millions of books available, you have chosen to learn how to carry your cross daily, and that is commendable. I hope this book has helped you deepen your connection with your faith and that you are now living a more Christ-like life. Remember, it's not enough to just read; we must put what we have learned into practice. With the strength and courage that comes from God, I am confident that you can do it!

I am eager to hear from you, whether in a letter or an email, about your experiences and your relationship with Jesus. I want to know what the Lord has been doing in your life and how you are growing as you carry your cross daily. Your feedback and experiences can be a source of inspiration for others on their spiritual journey.

Once again, thank you for reading this book. I am delighted to have been able to invite you to live authentically on your spiritual journey. Remember to find joy and delight in your new walk with Jesus.

Beloved, I pray that it may be well with you in all aspects of life and that you may continue to be in good health, just as your soul keeps thriving and prospering.

Have a great and blessed life!

Dr. Aigbefo D. Ehihi

REFERENCES

Barrett, Lois Y. *Treasure in Clay Jars: Patterns in Missional Faithfulness.* Grand Rapids, MI: Wm. Eerdmans Publishing Co., 2004.

Beard, Christopher. "Missional Discipleship: Discerning Spiritual-Formation Practices and Goals Within the Missional Movement." *Missiology* 43, no. 2 (Apr 2015): 175–94.

Beers, Holly. "Acts and the Servant. The Followers of Jesus as the 'Servant.'" *Luke's Model from Isaiah for the Disciples in Luke–Acts* (2015): 126–75.

Bosch, David J. *Transforming Mission: Paradigm Shifts in Theology of Mission.* Maryknoll: Orbis Books, 2016.

Dobbie, Robert. "*Canadian Journal of Theology: A Quarterly of Christian Thought* Vols 1 - 16 (1955 - 1970)." Biblical Studies.Org.UK, July 1958. https://biblical-studies.org.uk/articles_canadian-journal.php.

Frost, Michael, and Alan Hirsch. *The Shaping of Things to Come: Innovation and Mission for the 21st-Century Church.* Peabody, Mass.: Hendrickson, 2007.

Gelder, Craig Van, and Dwight J. Zscheile. *The Missional Church in Perspective: Mapping Trends and Shaping the Conversation.* Grand Rapids, MI: Baker Academic, 2011.

Gorman, Michael J. *Cruciformity: Paul's Narrative Spirituality of the Cross.* Grand Rapids, MI: Wm. B. Eerdmans Publishing Co., 2001.

Halter, Hugh, and Matt Smay. *And: The Gathered and Scattered Church* (Exponential Series). Grand Rapids, MI: Zondervan, 2010.

Haykin, Michael A. G. *The God Who Draws Near: An Introduction to Biblical Spirituality.* Webster, NY: Evangelical Press, 2007.

Hirsch, Alan, and Debra Hirsch. *Untamed: Reactivating a Missional Form of Discipleship.* Grand Rapids, MI: Baker Books, 2010.

Jacob, Edmund. *Theology of the Old Testament,* trans. Arthur W. Heathcote and Philip J. Allcock. New York: Harper and Row, 1958.

Johannes Lindblom, *The Servant Songs in Deutero-Isaiah. A New Attempt to Solve an Old Problem.* Lund: EWK. Gleerup, 1957.

Kline, Meredith G. *Genesis: A New Commentary,* Ed. Jonathan G. Kline. Peabody, MA: Hendrickson, 2017.

Lindblom, Johannes. *Prophecy in Ancient Israel.* Minneapolis: Augsburg Fortress Publishing, 1962.

Ludlow, Jared W. "Paul's Use of Old Testament Scripture," in *How the New Testament Came to Be.* Brigham Young University Religious Education Center, 2006. https://rsc.byu.edu/how-new-testament-came-be/pauls-use-old-testament-scripture.

Ludlow, Jared W. "ReligiousStudiesCenter." ReliefSocietyhttps://rsc.byu.edu/archived/selected-articles/paul-s-use-old-testament-scripture.

McClendon, Adam P., and Jared E. Lockhart. *Timeless Church: Five Lessons from Acts.* Nashville, TN: B & H Academic, 2020.

Maddix, Mark A. *Missional Discipleship: Partners in God's Redemptive Mission.* Kansas City, MO: Beacon Hill Press, 2013.

Miller, Stephen R. *Daniel.* Vol. 19, The New American Commentary: An Exegetical and Theological Exposition of Holy Scripture. Nashville: Broadman and Holman, 1994.

Murray, Andrew. *Humility.* Nashville: B&H Publishing Group, 2017.

North, Christopher R. *The Suffering Servant in Deutero-Isaiah. A Historical and Critical Study.* Oxford: Oxford University Press, 1956.

Nouwen, Henri J. M. *In the Name of Jesus: Reflections on Christian Leadership with Study Guide for Groups and Individuals.* New York: Crossroad Pub. Co. 2002.

Roberts Jr., Bob. *The Multiplying Church: The New Math for Starting New Churches.* Grand Rapids, MI: Zondervan, 2008.

Sheldrake, Philip. *Spirituality: A Brief History.* Malden, MA: Wiley-Blackwell, 2007.

Wilson, Todd. *Multipliers: Leading Beyond Addition.* N.p.: United States Exponential, 2017.

Whitney, Donald S. *Spiritual Disciplines for the Christian Life.* Colorado Springs, CO: NavPress, 2014.

Whitney, Donald S., and J. I. Packer. *Spiritual Disciplines for the Christian Life Study Guide.* Colorado Springs, CO: NavPress Publishing Group, 2014.

Wright, Christopher J. H. *The Mission of God: Unlocking the Bible's Grand Narrative.* Downers Grove: InterVarsity Press, 2006.

Wright, N. T. *Paul. In Fresh Perspective.* Minneapolis: Fortress Press, 2009.

ABOUT THE AUTHOR

Dr. Aigbefo D. Ehihi is an incredibly accomplished coach, pastor, and military chaplain with an exceptional track record of success that speaks for itself. With advanced education in theology, leadership, and social and behavioral sciences, he possesses an unparalleled depth of knowledge and expertise in his field. Driven by a divine calling, Dr. Ehihi, along with his wife and children, actively participates in ministry, and together, they are committed to uplifting and inspiring people. He is a highly respected author and leader known for his unwavering passion and dedication to sharing God's Word through active participation in Christian ministry and military service.

ABOUT THE BOOK

LIVING EVERY DAY WITH THE CROSS

If you are looking for a book that can help you deepen your connection to your faith and live a more genuine and meaningful Christian life, *Living Every Day with the Cross* by Dr. Aigbefo D. Ehihi is an excellent choice. This book explores genuine discipleship and the challenges Christ's followers face. Dr. Ehihi presents a comprehensive guide to the traits of a true disciple with practical tools for self-assessment and spiritual growth. *Living Every Day with the Cross* is infused with warmth, authenticity, and a genuine passion for helping readers navigate the complexities of discipleship. This book is a testament to faith, a celebration of Jesus, and an invitation to live authentically in your spiritual journey.

Other Books By Dr. Ehihi

AVAILABLE NOW!

A CALL TO FORGE
MEANINGFUL
CONNECTIONS

Unlocking the transformative power of connectivity

DR. AIGBEFO D. EHIHI

Notes

www.ingramcontent.com/pod-product-compliance
Lightning Source LLC
Chambersburg PA
CBHW060911120626
46553CB00001B/284